Panacea Poetry

Written & Illustrated by

Bethany Johnson

Copyright © 2023 Bethany Johnson.
All rights reserved.

No part of this book can be reproduced in any form or by written, electronic or mechanical, including photocopying, recording, AI or by any information retrieval system without written permission in writing from the publisher.

Published by Books by Sarah
www.booksbysarah.co.uk

ISBN 9798856106656

Dedication

For beautiful wild-thing Reuben - who was unwell in bed when I became committed to completing this work.

There is no love more potent than the love we cherish for our children. I could not have loved anything more than when I held you poorly in my arms and cried to see you suffer.

This book was an act of dedication to your wellbeing.
May your life be rich with health & love (the greatest treasures),
& may all children be guided to a space of happiness & health
as Humankind rekindles a conscious,
compassionate connection with nature & each other.

In dark times, we can be the light.

Foreword

This is my beautiful daughter Beth. Welcome to her treasured work 'Panacea Poetry'.

This cherished collection comes to you in two parts; the first, while born of a deep spiritual belief, also blossomed from a simple wish for love and gentle kindness, and to impart the healing power of nature. The clarity and simplicity of word conveys precious messages including peace in authenticity, wisdom in learned experience, beauty in everything and everyone, and above all else, the value of health and love.

Beth's writing was a craft well-honed, and her art also demonstrates an intense depth and desire for meaning - even within pieces created when she was a child. The second part of the book, 'Growing Up', has been gathered from poetry written during her teenage years. This part of the book includes the poem 'God Bless my Happy Nightmare' for which she won 'The John Clare Prize for Poetry' in 2011 at the age of just 14, and which she delivered in Westminster Hall. Beth was always very serene and humble, and tended to shy away from the limelight, so it was a joy to learn that she had told her brother how proud she continued to be of this huge achievement.

When she shared the first draft of 'Panacea Poetry' with me in 2018, I was impressed with the quality of the writing. However, the true meaning, wisdom and force of positive energy did not resonate until I revisited it after her death. During her final months, she worked so hard to complete the poetry collection, and lovingly assembled it alongside her art in a sketchbook. What a delight it was to find that this sumptuous work was complete - it has given me so much pleasure to publish it for her.

I hope Beth is pleased with the result - I think it is stunning, (but of course, I am her very proud mum!) Her words of wisdom, kindness and hope bring me so much comfort - and it is her deepest wish to reach out to you too.

Love and Light,

Sarah (Mother of Bethany Johnson), August 2023

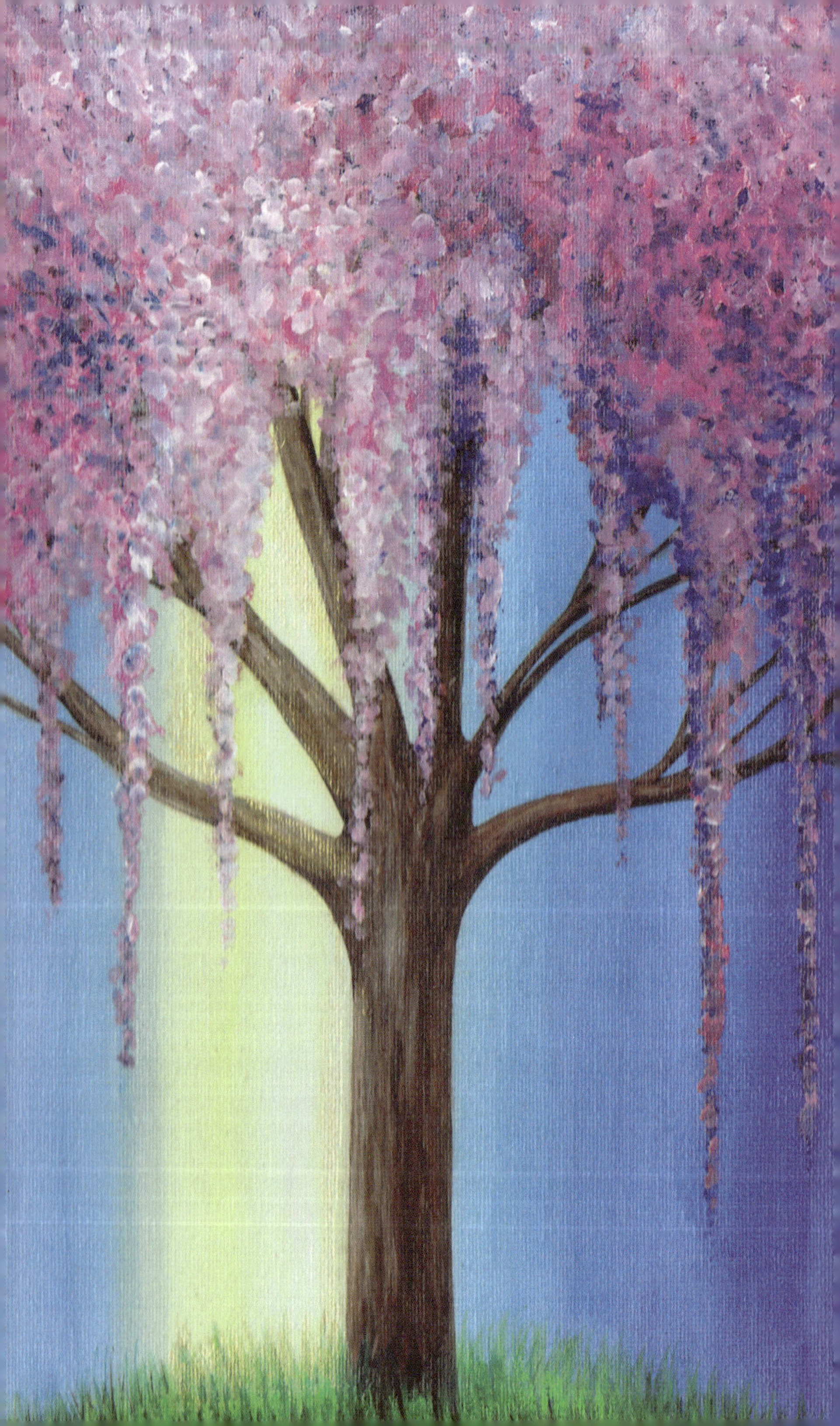

Panacea Poetry

Art 1

The Beauty of Human Form 3

Lucidity 5

Pandemic of Spiritual-Amnesia 7

Oasis 9

Birth: Divine Origins 13

Soul 16

Shattered Illusions 21

The Reality of Perfection 25

Karmic Knot 27

Lies 30

Lovable 39

The Lamb Transformed to Wolf 43

Awareness 47

The Riddle of Multiple Truths 49

Mother's Prayer 53

Truest Love 59

Truly Golden 63

Beautiful reader, I desire to seduce your heart,
mind & soul with pure words woven from dreams,
enchantment & all that I am.

I feel intense pleasure & gratitude that you're here in this moment,
devoting attention to creative writing
that begged to be birthed & I reach out lovingly to you.

Bethany ♡ Johnson

my study of 'Adam and Eve' by Raphael

Art

It is a magical joy to channel self-expression into Art.

All Art is born of self-expression,

therefore Art is intensely personal:

a sacred portal into another perspective.

Panacea Poetry by Bethany

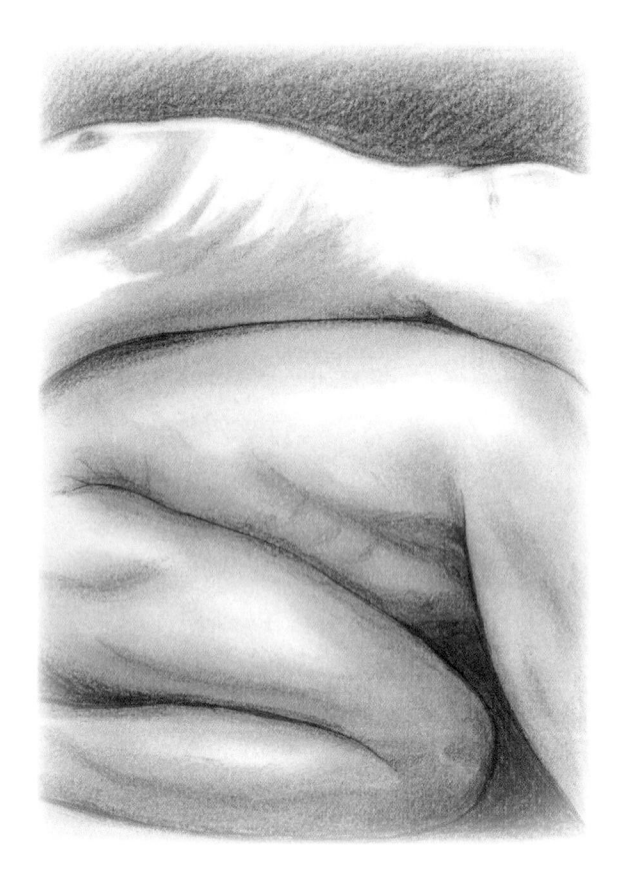

The Beauty of Human Form

Carve me from the movements of my body
& how I consciously choose to treat myself.

Let blood rush like pristine rivers flow
& muscle form with titanium strength.

Serenade the contours of my shape
so they're silken to your touch.

Let my hair be full of Vitality's kiss
as it tickles your face & cascades to my waist
- a veil embracing us.

Your hands steady me as we spin in a vortex of our own.
Energy blocks melt away: ice in the sun's heat.

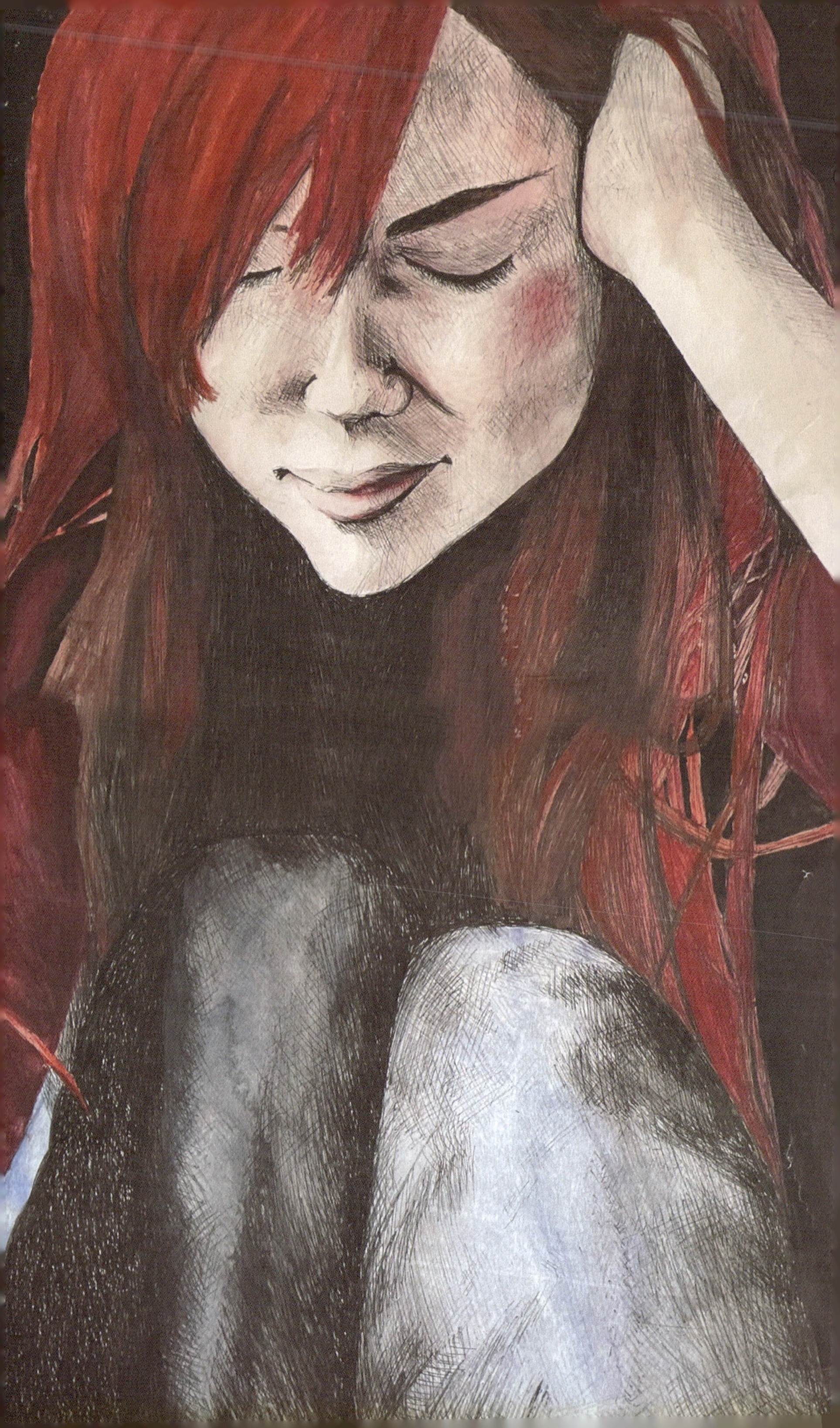

In Dark Times We Can Be The Light

Lucidity

In her awakening she saw that her dreams were real
- her nightmares too -

but that the truest illusion was the lie that she was powerless.
She saw now that the power was hers.

All she had to do was remember.

Remember who she was.

Remember who she was becoming.

Remember what she came here to do.

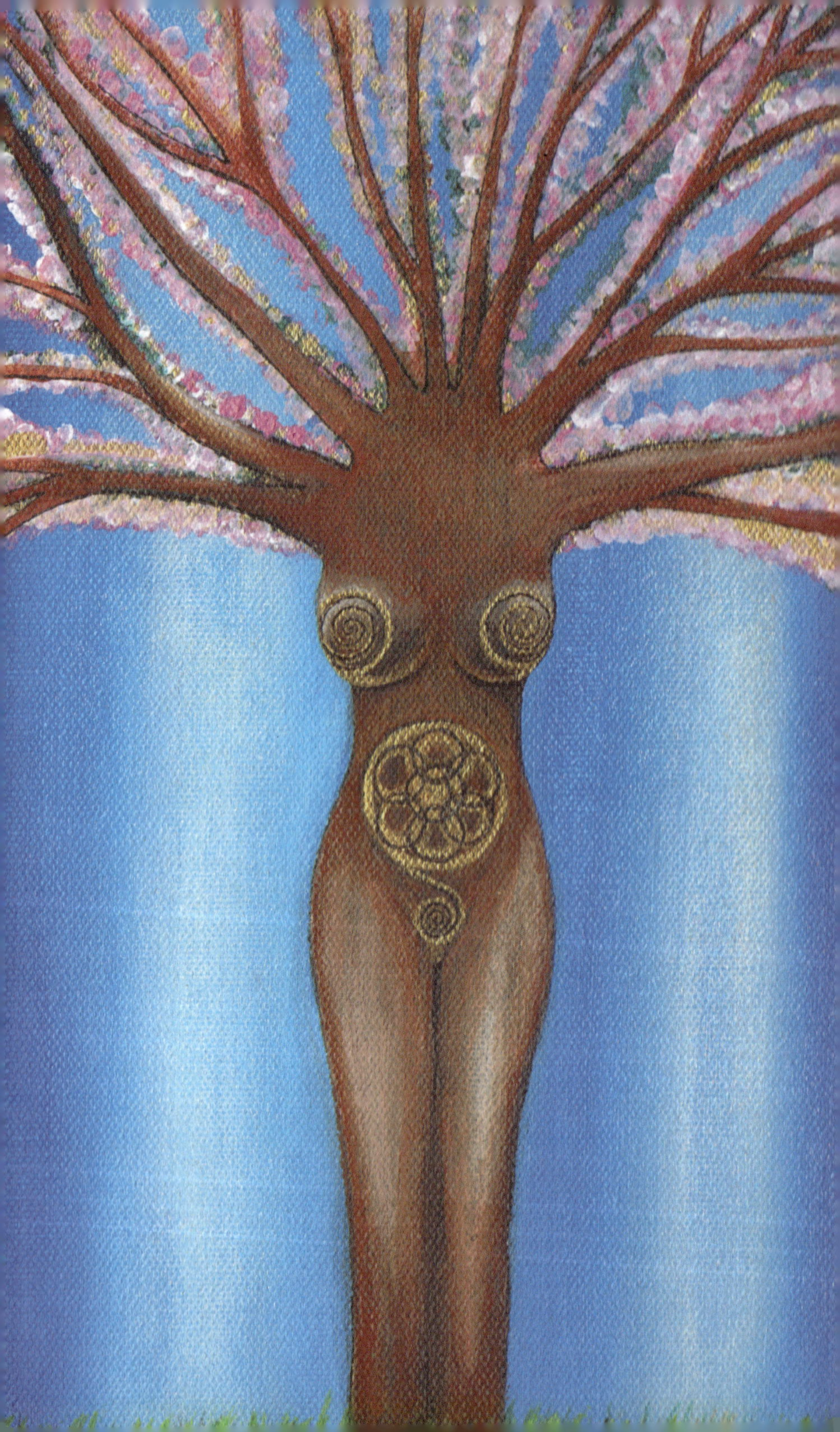

Pandemic of Spiritual-Amnesia

Spiritual amnesia is forgetting your eternal soul was born of
the same stream as all that surrounds you.

An essence inextricably connected to yours
flows throughout consciousness:
eternal, celestial, indestructible -
an alchemical flame burning brightly.

This radiance can be obscured from sight
by torment, hatred, fear and deception.

Nonetheless, this magic exists within & around you - always.

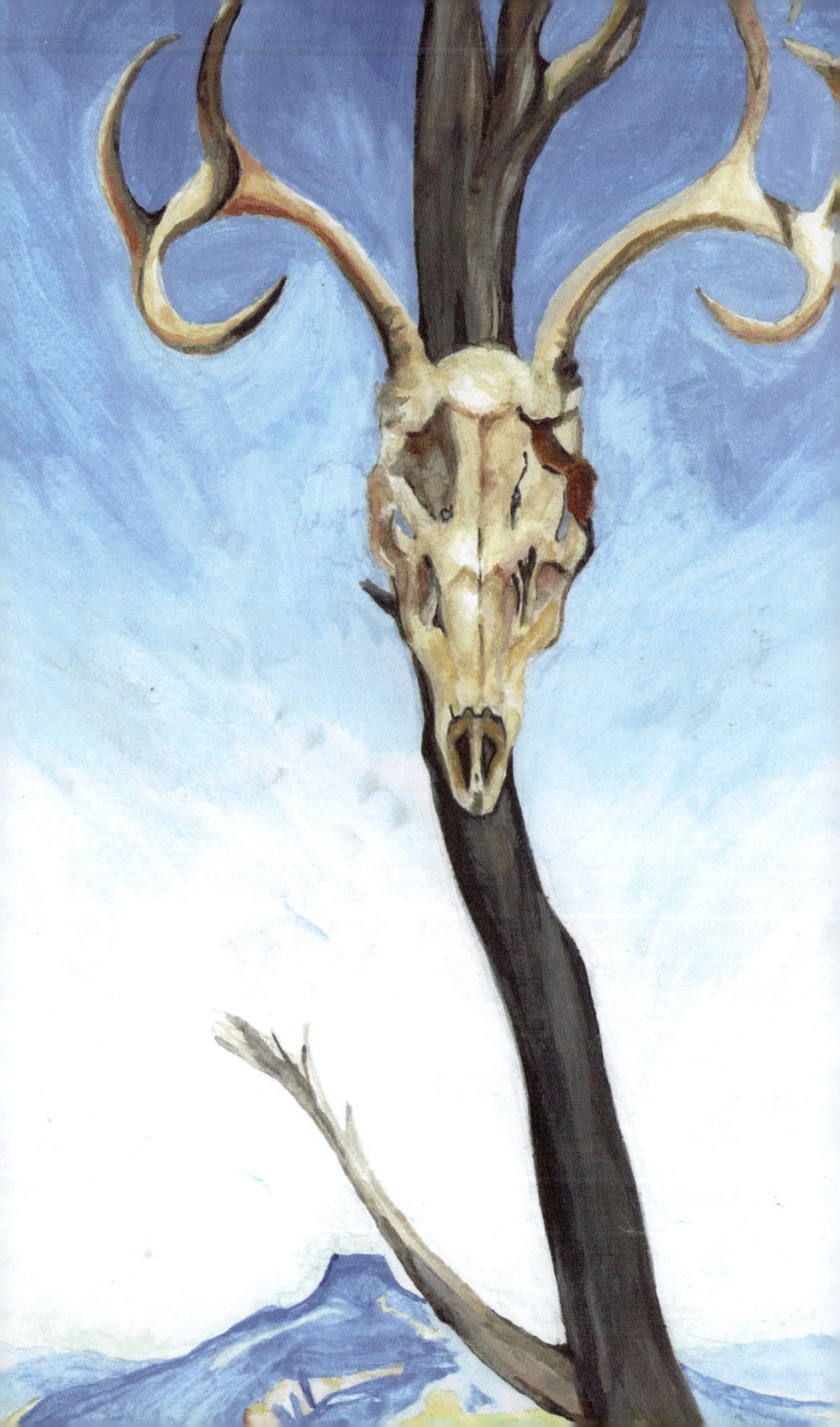

Oasis

From a damaged body, hurt heals.
From a tormented mind, pain births acute awareness.
From an aching heart, you will be blissfully whole.
Miles of trauma - knotted & twisted tightly in your frame -
are stripped to cinders & carried away,
on a breeze that leaves behind
the nectar-sweet, summer scent of new promises.

For the fragments of you that thirsted with chapped lips,
a diamond-pure pool overflows with unconditional love & presence
- a holy grail which never leaves you empty;
an elixir which never makes you choke.
This Ormus seeps through blood - flooding veins, arteries;
embracing & beautifying scars.
Your metamorphosis has only just begun.

In a burnt-ochre desert devoid of life,
an expansive oasis seeps from Terra's breasts;
nurturing emerald-green seedlings into fertile, fruit-bearing trees.
Lagoon-blue waterfalls plunge over boulders,
oxygenating the root systems of tropical foliage;
transforming the habitat from hopelessness to sanctuary.

From the murky-grey toxicity of a polluted concrete jungle,
- where poverty, sickness, conflict & crime are siblings to one another-
a thought becomes a prayer;
the whisper of a healing revolution on the air.
A collaboration of creative hands transform deficient earth into rich soil.
The challenge of dedication & effort despite difficulty
does not compare to the desolation of abandoning hope.

We collaborate together,
setting aside the conflicts that seek to weaken us.
We may not all be united in friendship,
but we possess a shared, greater purpose.
The potent blood of a Human flows through all our veins.
Each of us bare unique scars from the lessons life bestows.
Each individual is a treasure-trove of experience.

Panacea Poetry by Bethany

In Dark Times We Can Be The Light

Our resourcefulness, best efforts & committed conscious-awareness
gift a harvest of empowerment & environmental-beautification;
setting the long-awaited societal, energetic shift into motion.
Heirloom seeds become abundant, organic delights of vibrant colour.
Flowers of fuschsia, lavender, violet, sunflower-yellow, daisy-white,
clementine & poppy-red spread tantalizingly,
as a bee's fragrant paradise across roof tops, balcony gardens,
hanging baskets & support frames secured to brick and fence.

Where animals are raised for foods,
they are nurtured with respect & sacrificed with an understanding
that their sacred body has been taken for nourishment,
and all parts of their body shall be honoured
as the animal's spirit becomes free in Death.

Our purpose expands beyond ourselves.
We are bound to one another on a healing adventure to greater Love.

Are your eyes open yet?

Even a blind man can see, when his mind is opened.
Even a blind man can see, when his heart is healed.

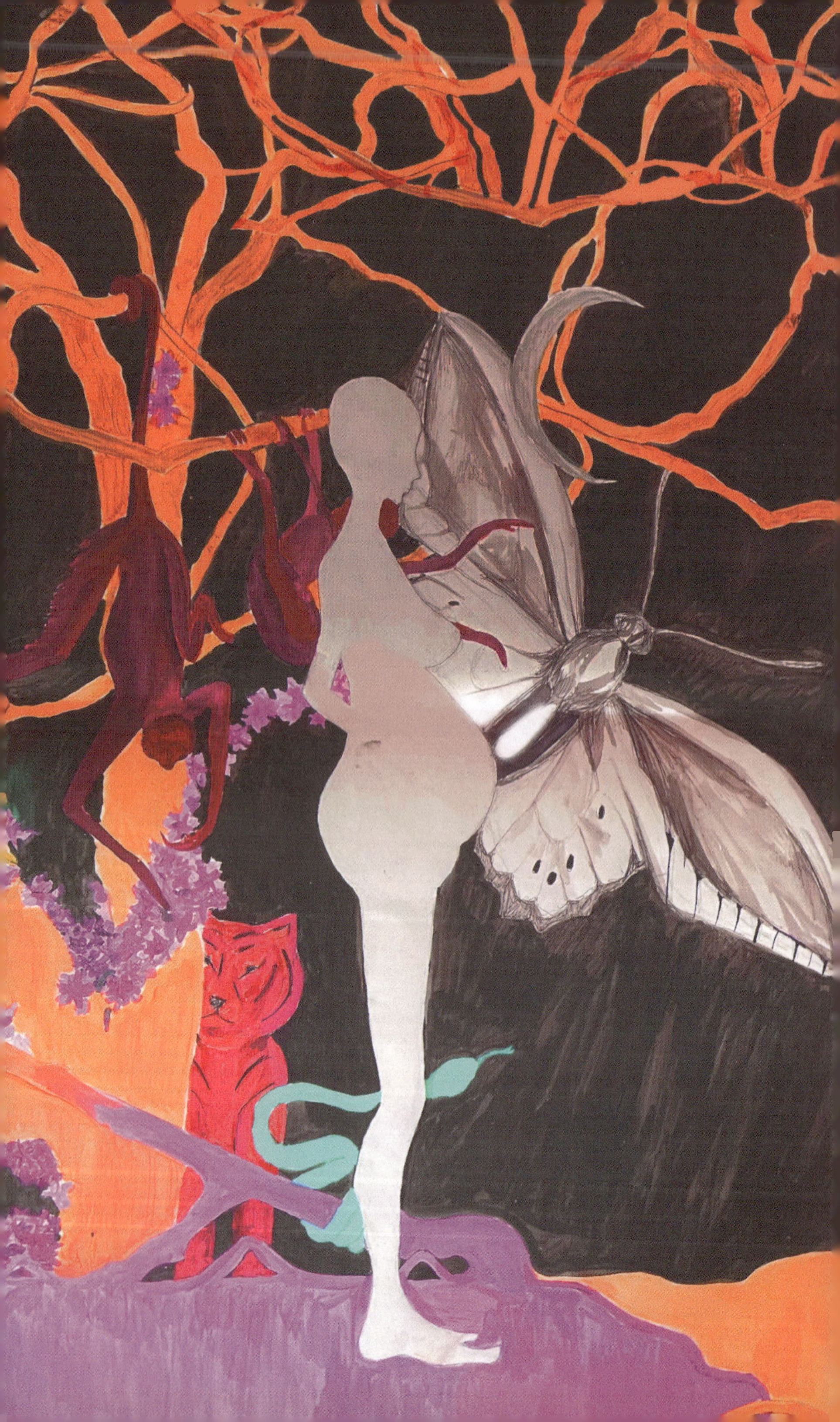

Birth:
Divine Origins

The trauma of Birth
- the shocking sensation of separation -
overwhelms your new body.

You are naked in raw emotion.
The shivers of biting cold awaken your first warrior-cry,
before the all-embracing heat of breast and blanket
can clutch you intensely to life.

Loving connection is as vital as oxygen
through this transition from the womb that was your sanctuary,
to your guardian's gentle arms.
An entire world is spiralling around you -
awed by the undeniable reality of your existence.

You are a magnet for all the attention in the room.
The flame of your vibrant heart is urged to keep beating.
Those tiny, valiant lungs are urged to keep breathing.
Those deep, enchanting eyes are urged to keep confirming

- 'I am alive.'

Panacea Poetry by Bethany

In Dark Times We Can Be The Light

On this day, time is not applicable -
because you have ripped all focus from it.
You have already begun altering the course of the future forever,
so immense is your value.
Temporary amnesia,
but the thought always resides somewhere inside...

You were born of strongest seed & strongest egg colliding in ecstasy;
nurtured by a womb that shed & quickened passionately for you.
A spiralling, ethereal energy weaved your eternal essence
from threads of divine artistry.

Fire, Water, Earth, Metal, Air, Ice

- the elements of life pour vivaciously
in a scientifically ingenious union;
overspilling like warm, wet, woman's milk.

Soul

A gleaming, glistening angel-light,
expectant for human-form
- in ether where all time & no time passed at all.
Your full power is a patient Deity,
yearning for you to unleash its panacea.

Death is not what you have perhaps thought or been taught.
Life is constant potential & will always be accessible to you.

When one path ends,
a multitude of new paths are offered to you.

No path is ever lost -
only another golden key in your soul evolution & ancestry.

In Dark Times We Can Be The Light

You are attached to the character you play,
the body-vessel you align with.
Perhaps you forget that you are not just your body
- or your mind.

There is much more available in your future,
& much more magic to your origins
than you may currently realise.

This will change.

Panacea Poetry by Bethany

In time, you will remember your divine truth.
The ones you love will never be truly lost to you.

Death is an illusion.

The truth is both beautiful and comforting.
If you seek truth & are fully open,
it cannot be kept from you.

The pace of your evolution will always be a gentle one.
Do not be afraid if others seem further ahead than you or superior to you.
It is simply not true.
You are exactly where you should be.

Through all the pains we cannot understand,
clarification will dawn.

In Dark Times We Can Be The Light

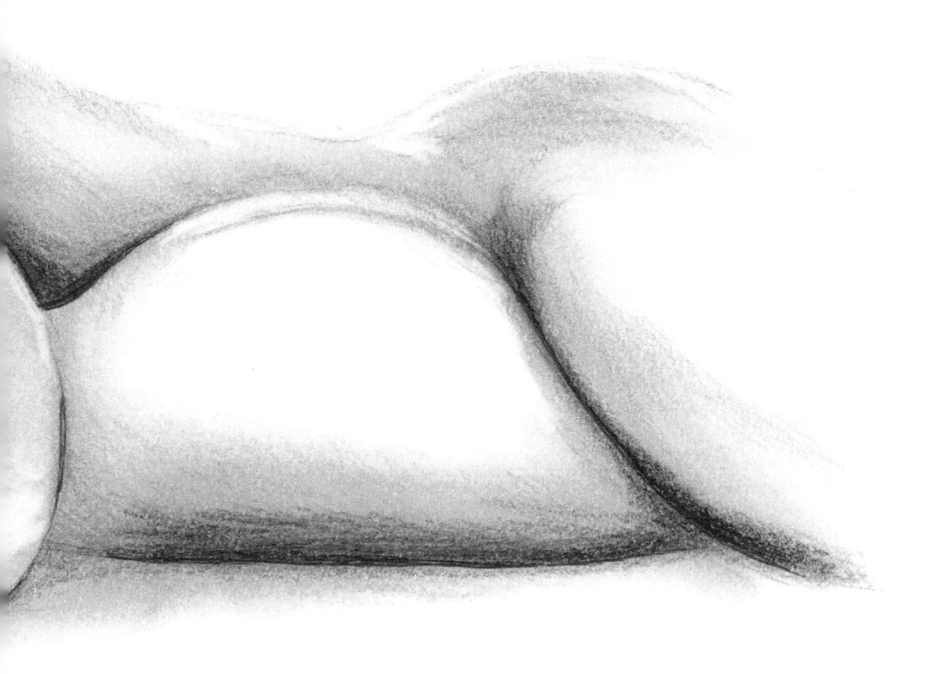

We each have our talents
as well as aspects of us which are in the process of strengthening.

You are exactly appropriate for your journey.

How can someone with a different body,
a different collection of experiences, a different purpose
know what is better for you, than you do?

How can they know what you should or should not be?

Abandon expectation and devote yourself to true love.

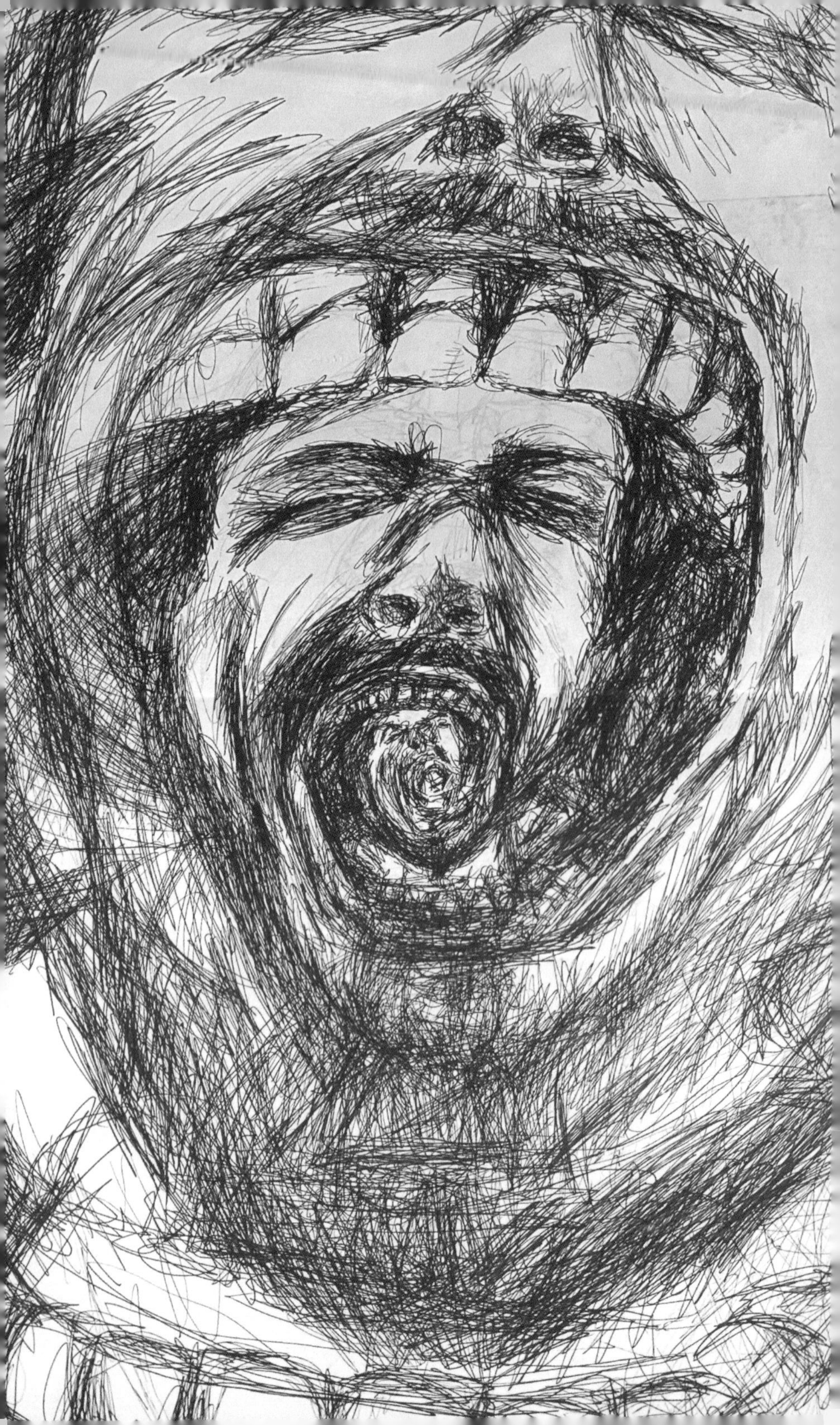

Shattered Illusions

I have been pushed into a corner
& expectations thrust on me
to be terribly 'normal'; a calm, quiet, contained 'good girl.'
(See me be seen and not heard,
my broken-self performs this beautifully).

I have been forced into a character
that was the 'correct' one to play
& told to reject everything else that I am.
(One face for all of mankind).
Slowly we are all transforming: lifeless, inhibited zombies.
(See us cannibalize our creative authenticity).

Yes, my head is in the clouds,
but it gives me a 'higher perspective'.
How can you justly crucify a character expression,
when all personalities have negative & positive polarities?
Your capacity for personal development,
learning & compassion is intimately tied
to your mind & heart's capacity to be open.

It has become strange to be insane;
yet, it is insane to be so much of the same.

I refuse to be what you expect of me.
My character & definition of self
is ripping violently from the inside outwards.
I had been blind to the shards embedded in my skin,
but now I tear them from me piece by piece
& feel the orgasmic release.

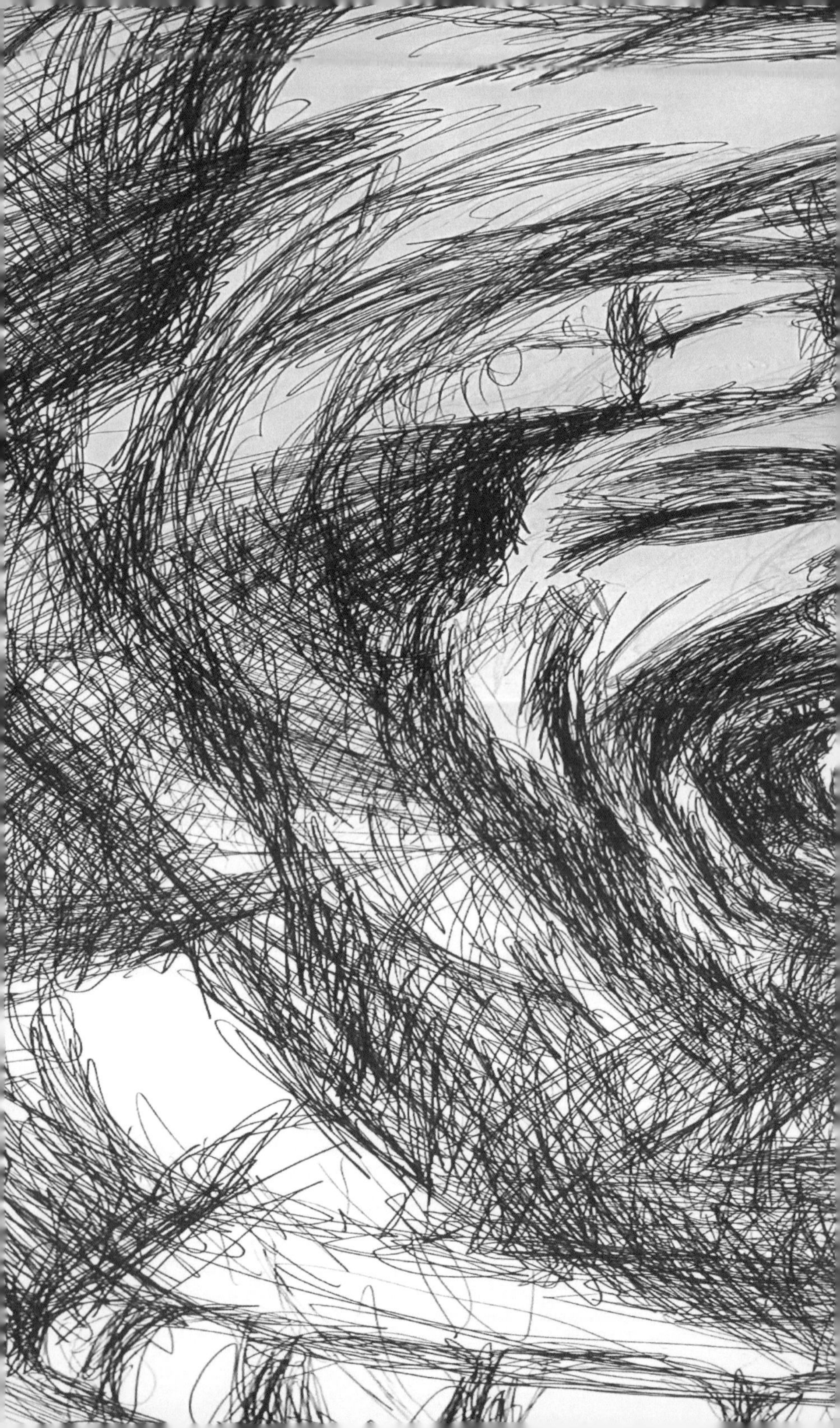

I am all things & nothing
& all things & nothing is real.
Life is an illusion -
& I shatter it like the fake reflection in your eyes.
I own many faces - magnificent masks -
& behind them, my etheric energy rides life.

You want me to be mundane
because insanity threatens to awaken your zombie-brain...
lucidity is drugging & awakening me.

Lucidity laughs obscenely & dances - deliriously drunk -
as Truth dawns - vivid as a ruby-sun's flames spill across the sky...

Life is a play, and we are a part of the breath of its becoming.

Panacea Poetry by Bethany

The Reality of Perfection

If you are always wearing masks,
people can only ever fall in love with a mask.
If someone doesn't love you for the real you,
then you deserve better.

We deserve to be loved for the authenticity of us.
We deserve to not feel compelled
to constantly alter our behaviours & identity
according to the unkind expectations of others.

Our definition of the word 'perfection' needs to be critically analysed.
In its archaic form 'perfection' is glorified as the ideal state;
a space free from 'fault' or 'mistake.'
However, a world without mistake
would be a world devoid of growth & learning,
a world without possibility & self-expansion.

Mistakes are a catalyst for wisdom: beautiful stepping stones
in a realm of constant evolution & exploration.

It is a positive, possible thing,
to leave behind the things which don't love us the way we deserve,
no matter how terrifying or impossible that sometimes feels.

Give yourself the opportunity to embrace life
by abandoning the destructive, futile expectation of 'perfection.'

In this way, the door of self-love & joyful living can be opened.

Panacea Poetry by Bethany

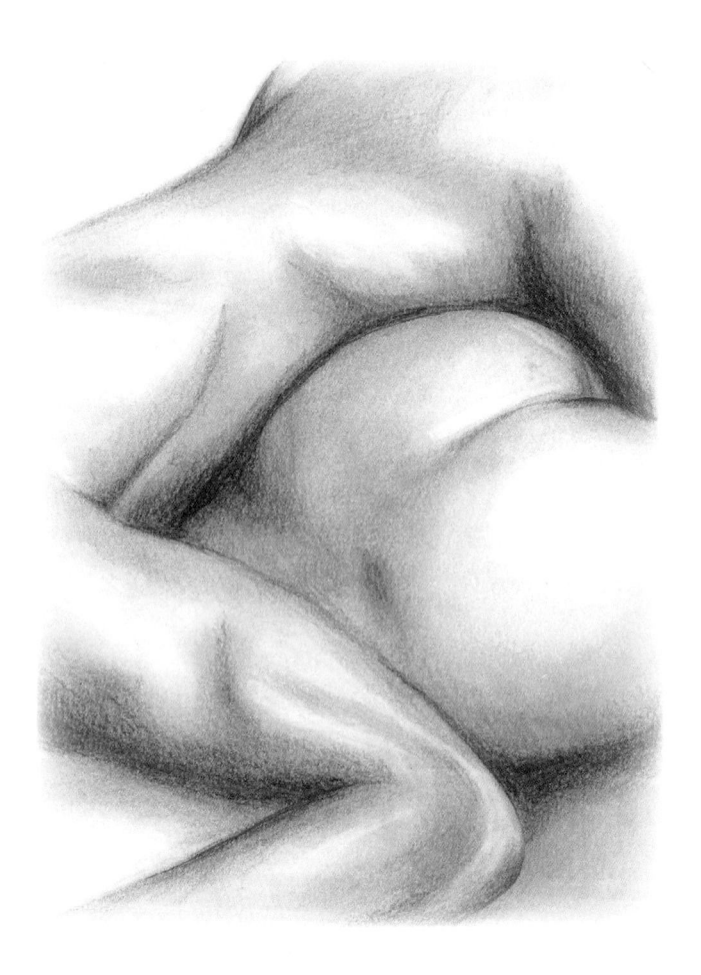

Karmic Knot

To hurt another is to self-harm
& to self-harm is to hurt another.

To spill blood when your body does not need to take blood
is to taint your own life's blood.

To be sadistic towards the others who inhabit this realm,
is like punching the reflection in the mirror,
to find the shattered shards slash into your own fists,
yet not comprehending how your action caused your pain.

The sword you wield cannot cut another
without slicing you in karmic exchange.
Whether you feel the pain or flee from it,
the bitter aftertaste lingers:
a poison slowly setting in your veins.

To hurt another is to self-harm
and to self-harm is to hurt another.

Notes:

As a child, I perceived Karma as being punished for bad behaviour, or rewarded for good behaviour. As children we grow up being taught about the witch who turned an egotistical, handsome prince into a Beast for his cruelty; only the development of humility alongside compassionate love for others can redeem him.

However, Karma is not intended to be a punishment. It is intended to be a learning tool that highlights this truth: we are inescapably, intimately linked to the rest of the universe. Each action we take is a pebble (or a boulder) in a pool - causing ripples to expand outwards. Our thoughts, words, actions or inaction set in motion consequences, the scope of which we are rarely fully aware.

In Greek Mythology, Helios 'the sun God' is responsible for guiding the sun across the sky each day. He pulls the sun with a golden chariot led by flying horses. When Helios allows his son Phaethon (born of a human mother) to ride the chariot instead of him (without experience or correct training), Phaethon becomes overwhelmed & terrified by the sight of the earth so far below & the stars so near, which causes him to lose control of the horses. Consequently, the sun is brought too close to the earth. The intensity of the heat sets fields of crops aflame, makes the seas boil and scars vast areas of land into desert. Zeus, the thunder God, intervenes by striking Phaethon from the sky & to his death in order to stop all of Earth from being scorched by fire. With Phaethon gone, the horses begin to calm and resume their regular journey across the sky.

Hearing this story, we understand that if Phaethon & Helios had been better prepared & less reckless, the outcome of the experience would have been radically different.

It is the consequences of the decisions we make which become our greatest teachers. It is this life experience, and how we react to it, that shapes us into the people we become. Karma is an intrisic part of the pact of being alive in this realm, the golden key in an inevitable cycle of metamorphosis.

Therefore, I no longer perceive Karma as a punishment or something to be feared (as I did when I was a girl). It is simply an indication of the potential power you have in whatever you do. A catalyst for personal development, Karma gives individuals an immense amount of control into shaping the kind of life they desire for themselves. We have a direct sense of responsibility for many of the happenings that occur in our lives & future. We are weaving our own fates.

In Dark Times We Can Be The Light

What will you do with your power? The voice, choice, body, feeling, thought, dreams, wealth, faith that are yours? Your power can help to shape the future of humanity and our world into something outstandingly beautiful ('what is an ocean but a multitude of drops?'-Cloud Atlas).

If you envision your life as a temple, realize the pillars supporting this temple are your health. If you forge them from diamonds, you will embody divinity and titan-strength to the core. In this way, your life becomes a peaceful sanctuary of gemstone; a secret garden of abundance planted in golden soil. Strong roots stand fast against tempestuous storms.

But build the pillars of your temple from rotten wood, neglect the plants, lace the water with venom... the toxicity would weaken you; your temple would crumble to dust - a broken shell where nothing grows.

Your body is a gift, constantly working to regenerate and enhance itself. Your body is a miracle... but it is not indestructible & requires conscious awareness of correct care..

Sickness is a painful, piteous place, in alignment with self-hate; that's why we care what is on our plate. It's why we care about the air we breathe & why we let ourselves recuperate & sleep. It's why we end abuse - speak out the truth.

Build barriers by making a commitment to self-love each day.

Lies

You are being lied to.
Sexism, objectification, suppression:
the darkness of humanity's obsession is toxicity in 'beauty' standard,
poisoning women with lies that their true form is less than perfection.

Shame, shame, shame to the girl, the mother, daughter, sister.
Shame for who they are & how their body isn't.
What greater pain than thinking something is wrong with us;
that we're less lovable in our natural state?

You are being lied to:
"Disgusting, dirty, here's a razor for your birthday,"
to the girls - before they're old enough to create a baby.
"You want to be sexy, don't you?"

Society whispers, malicious demolition
of pride, self-love & innocent self-appreciation:
"be as we say you should be,
this is the way beauty must be.
We will control you because
we can hurt you, judge you, insult you, mock you."

Then our children will be bullies too-
Bullies or hating themselves, or both.
Thus the sickness continues-
a monster with an insatiable appetite
paving the path to self-destruction
as we twist ourselves into painful forms
so we may be more accepted by others.

In Dark Times We Can Be The Light

This is not real love.
This is abuse.

Women were not created for men's pleasure;
to live a lie that we stay girls forever.
Our bodies are blossoming into their next seasons;
changing like the tides of a pearl moon.
That is beautiful too.

Panacea Poetry by Bethany

In Dark Times We Can Be The Light

A cycle spinning in multiple directions-
suppression & objectification
are not limited to feminine expression.
Society casts shame on a man's natural state;
forgetting that Samson's strength was that he never shaved.
A beard so long, and seven golden braids.

Norse God Odin, thick hair like a silver cloud,
charges his eight-legged horse across the sky.
Native American Warriors
ride barebacked on wild horses, spirits free;
hair ebony flames in the wind.
Ancient Samurai, Japanese warlords - hair uncut.

Blessed Jesus, Lamb of God - hair uncut.
Sacred journey from boy to man.
Don't let them steal your power child
by cropping yours & telling you
'that makes you more of a man'.

Panacea Poetry by Bethany

In Dark Times We Can Be The Light

Nature would grow hair tumbling down your back:
auburn-fire, copper-chestnut, honey-blond,
chocolate-brown, raven-black, moonshine-white, steel-grey.
Curls that bounce or strands that stream.

When you cut your hair - when you do anything -
do it not because you have to, do it only if you want to.

Nature knows man is beautiful and strong.
Nature knows man is power; man is glory.
Nature knows boy is the dawn of man.
Nature doesn't separate
the beauty from boy and the strength from girl.
Nature wills both to be embodied
by our essence and physical forms.

If society is sick, it does not make sense to conform
to society's definition of perfection.

Let us not feed the monster,
but help it to heal from the beast it has become.

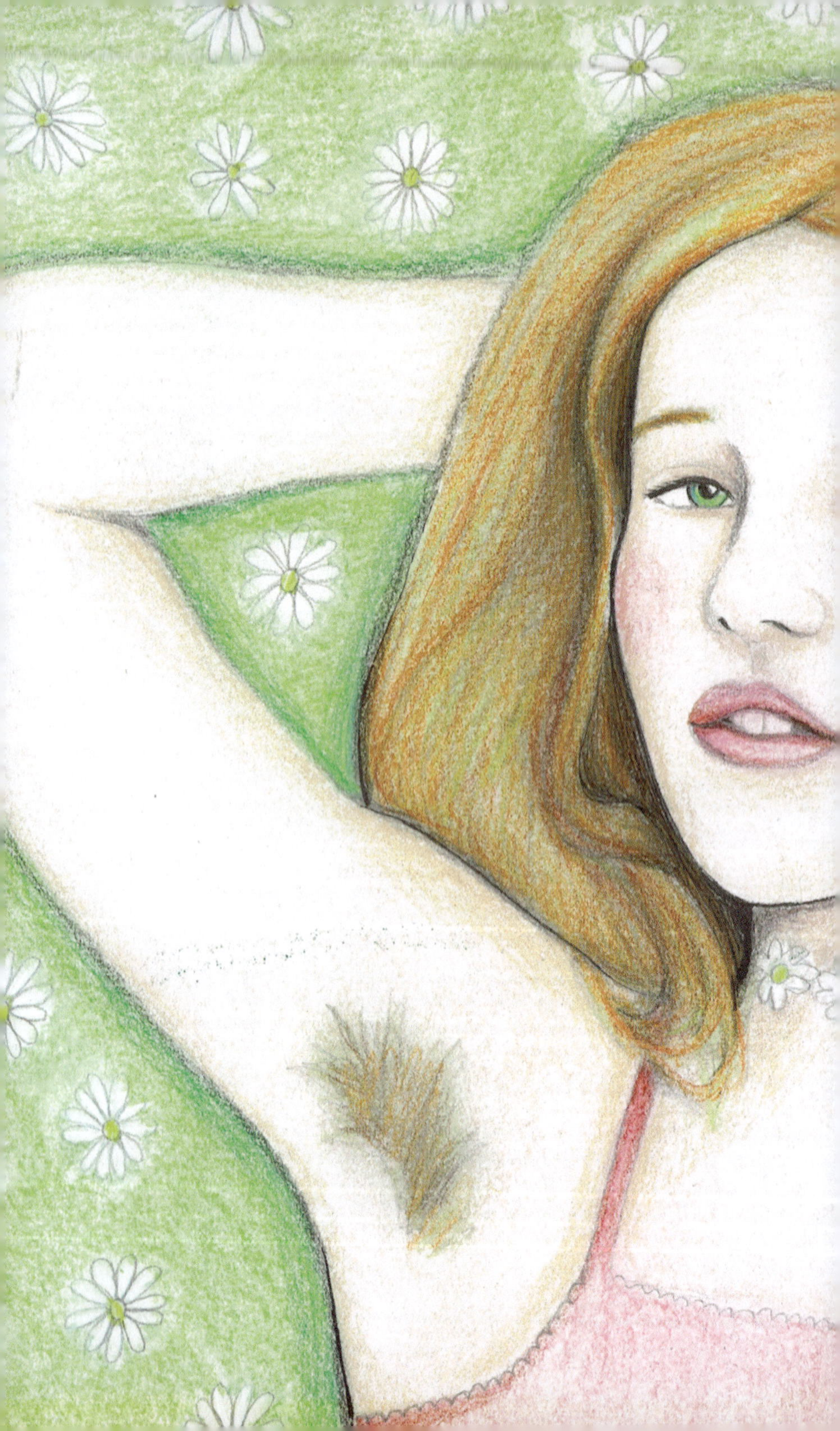

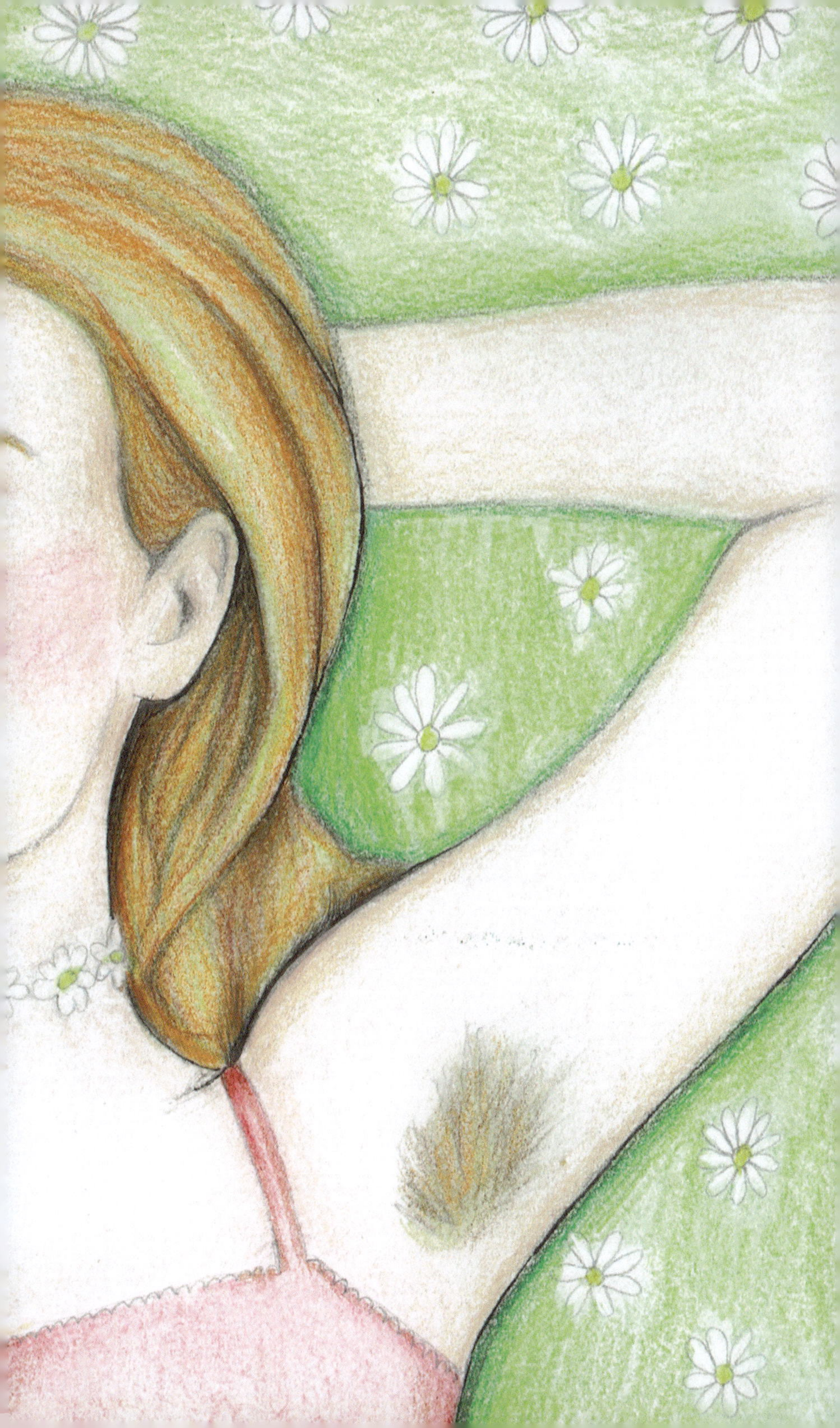

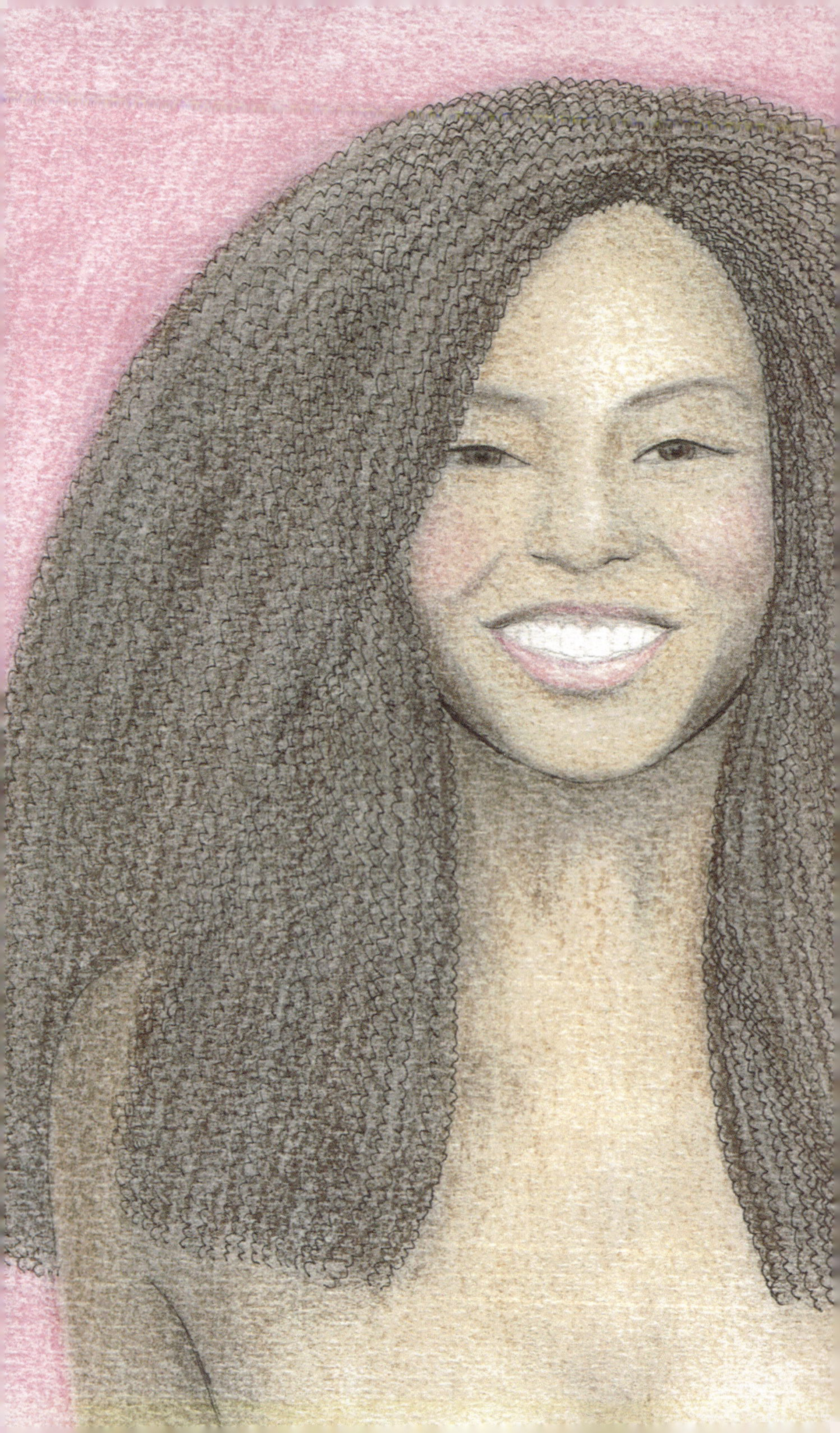

Lovable

I see a light in you,

that has been longing to be felt.

I see an artist in you,

that has been longing to create.

I see a pain in you,

that has been longing to be held.

I see an intensity in you,

that tells me your emotions have taken you places

where you've felt alone in your pain.

I want to take that away

& flood you with the knowing

that angels hold you

& fae dance around you in the woods.

I want you to know you're lovable

& easy to love.

Panacea Poetry by Bethany

May angel wings lift your spirit & send it soaring.

May the might of God break the chains which bind you.

May hurt heal into joyous gifts.

When you're sat within the trees,

all the spirits of the forest recognize their kin.

You have fae blood, human.

You have taken a journey

so you may grow,

but at home with the fae is your world.

They take you,

they teach you,

they caress you;

angels love you.

Until the time when you step through a portal & find yourself home,

hear them singing in the distance;

close your eyes & let Gaia be your guide.

Golden light floods you, stitching up open wounds;

regenerating the beautiful truth of you.

Panacea Poetry by Bethany

The Lamb Transformed to Wolf

Sometimes we don't know we will never go back,

or see a person or place again - we just never do.

We grow apart from the person we used to be

and in the art of healing - find ourselves transformed;

incompatible with the life we used to know.

Metamorphosis - I have been shaped.

I always loved butterflies.

There are some pains you can't experience

and remain the same.

Some lessons irrevocably alter your core coding;

some scars slice so potently you think you'll never heal,

but a miracle occurs and time shows you

stronger, wiser, kinder and healing still.

The places and loves I once lived -

so much of life is the art of letting go.

So much of my life has shown me what it means

to feel out of control;

how so many of us don't feel safe.

Safety is what we really need, not control.

In Dark Times We Can Be The Light

My life is teaching me how to cast

the black & white flag of peace

& to be the dove flying with the breeze;

knowing it is leading me right where I need to be.

My life is teaching me to love & understand

that darkness & light are twins: hand in hand.

I know - have to believe -

that if I can comprehend those who hurt me;

& merge peace with the memory of them,

some immense power will be accessed.

Treasured wisdom will emerge;

turning weeping wound to indestructible diamond.

The vital knowledge that the ones who hurt me

grew me into what I am; who I want to be.

I am the lamb transformed into Wolf.

In this way, trauma is a gift.

Panacea Poetry by Bethany

Awareness

Loneliness, confusion, a lack of love,
self-hate and depression are states that exist within most of us,
whether short-lived or chronic.

We owe it to our humanity to broaden our minds and hearts
to realize that these pains exist.

When we collectively stop running away
or denying the existence of these states,
we can reach out and begin to heal.

Sometimes we put a lot of pressure upon one another.
We must not forget that we're each dealt different cards
through genetics and circumstance,
and all we can do is try our best with the hand we're dealt.

In this world, young people are particularly vulnerable.

We owe it to the children of our world to try and understand.

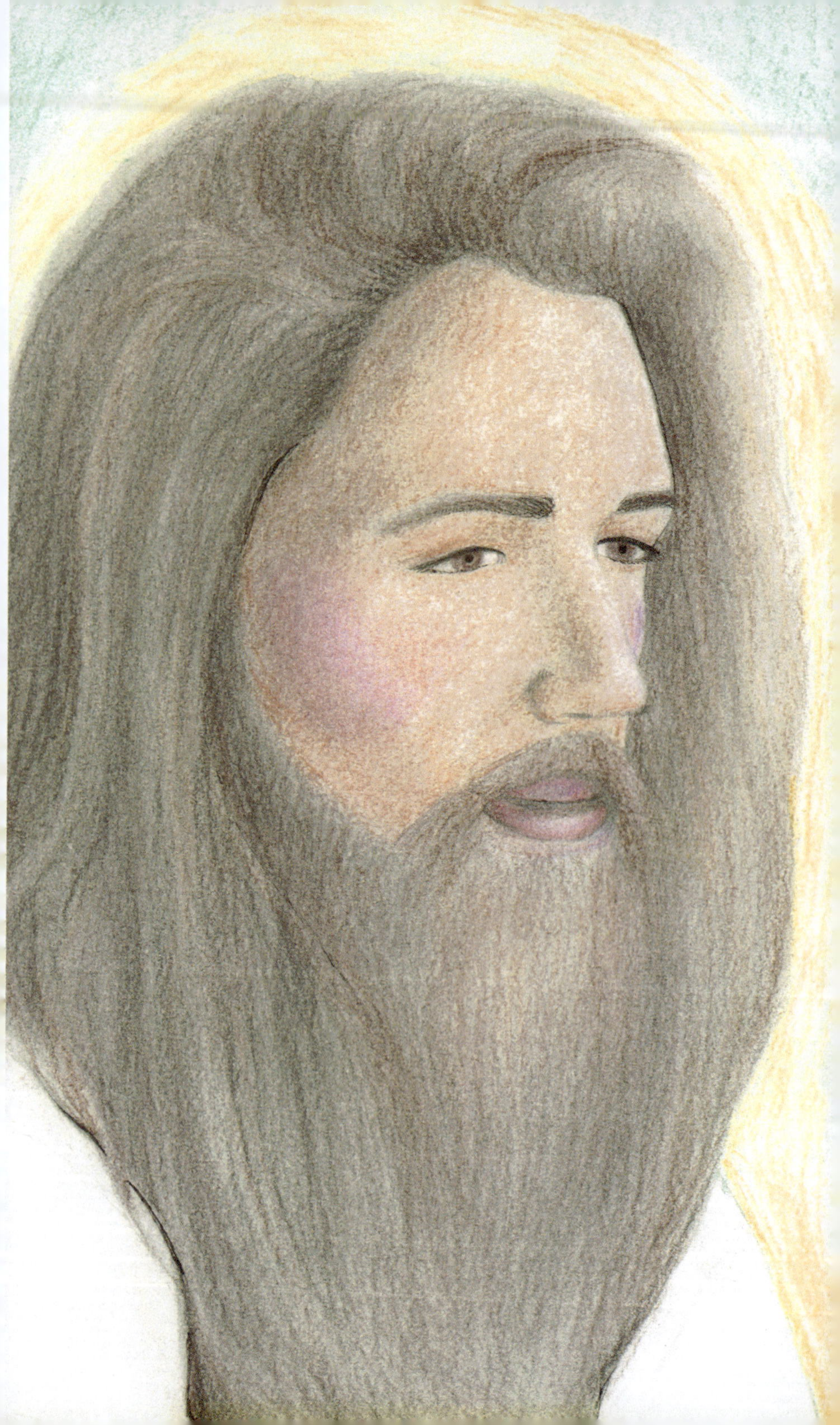

The Riddle of Multiple Truths

There is so much knowledge and information in this world.
Knowledge is a powerful, vital tool for self-expansion
and awareness of important matters.

Misinformation has potential for devastation.
Nothing feels worse than being misunderstood,
or told we are lying when we are authentically honest.

We have all had this experience.
Being heard and understood is so soothing.
Any burden becomes instantly lighter -
feels softer- when we are loved well.

Correct information is a bright light
to guide us through any labrynth.
However, sometimes the more we hunt
 and research outside of ourselves,
the more confused and seemingly lost we become.

The world is full of conflicting information.
Multiple truths exist simultaneously.

Truth can be a unique concept to a unique individual.
Too many people believe and preach their way
as the 'correct' universal truth.
Although many of us share certain basic truths,
the details of what is right and true for a person
varies greatly between us.

Panacea Poetry by Bethany

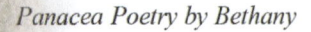

It is important to listen to and learn
a vast variety of information;
to grow our brains in new, exciting ways.
It is important to question
and re-evaluate what we think we know.
But there comes a time
when we must rest the researcher within us
- cease looking to the external world -
and instead look and feel within,
to the supreme guidance that already exists inside.

This guidance within us
is much more vast in its capacity
than our physical human-form.
We must learn to trust and seek our own guidance,
which is irreplaceable and of vital importance.

I promise all the answers you'll ever need
or want will find you ,
at exactly the right moment.
All you've ever desired to learn is waiting for you
- so long as you remain open-minded and open-hearted.

Do not seek to find only one correct way to live,
for if you do your search will be fruitless.
Remember you choose to exist in a world
that cannot be limited to that extent.

Moment to moment,
only ask yourself what feels loving to you,
and the surrounding world.

In Dark Times We Can Be The Light

Love is all you must learn and hold onto
whenever you are unsure of anything.

Love is your primary need.
Of no less value than food, water and warmth.
When you are starving of love, disease will grow.
When you replenish this fountain,
health will flourish.

Faith is a power that will work miracles.
Find anything that feeds you hope,
and hold on to it with everything you are.

You are exactly where you are supposed to be,
and on a journey to brighter places still.

Panacea Poetry by Bethany

Mother's Prayer

I pray day and night
to the sun, moon, stars
and to all the magical mystery of the universe.
Magic I know you hear and feel my desires.
Hear my powerful prayers
and deliver a responding, ever-burning golden light
to fulfil all my soul's desires.

Sweet angels, hear the purity of my wishes.
Please support me to grow in patience,
to speak with care, softness, kindness, understanding
and all that embodies the gentle,
divine feminine expressions of human nature.
Give me the gifts of awareness, strength and empathy
to speak and act not from anger or fear,
but from the highest forms of love and bravery.

May all the past lessons of my ancestors live within my essence
and reveal themselves through my choices.
Give me the wisdom to admit to hurt,
or ask for support from other humans
in the times where I struggle to embody this love.
Give me the strength to do what is right in how I raise my child,
even when the right choices aren't always the easiest.

I wish to nurture my child with pure foods and pure thoughts.
I wish to encourage a love of being within nature
- lively feet on leaves,
fingertips touching the bark of trees,
the sun kissing their soft skin.

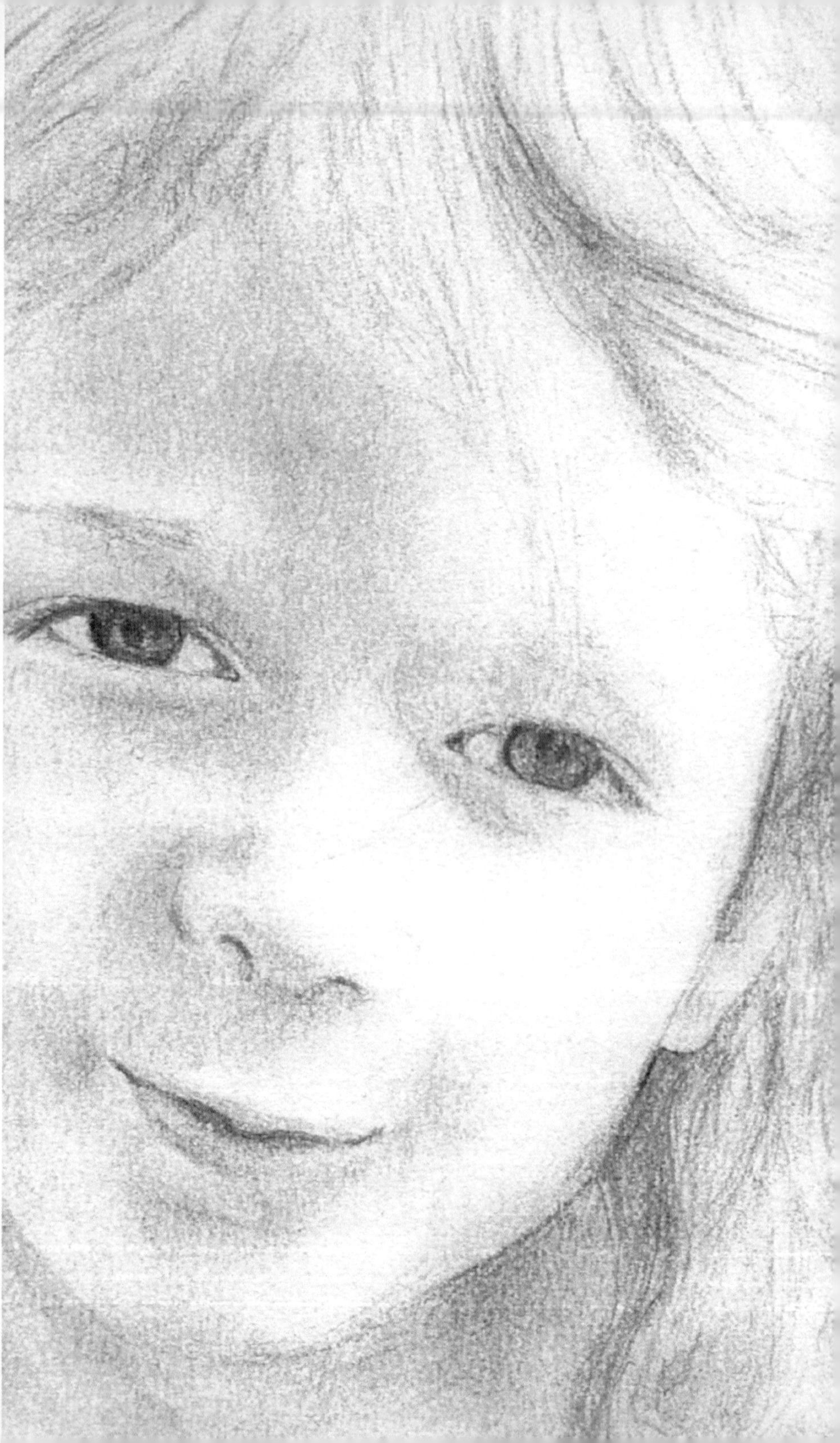

In Dark Times We Can Be The Light

Our children are all cherubic-innocence
as they first taste the rain, dance in a storm,
see spring relinquish the cold of winter,
and transform the scenery into vibrant new beginnings.
We see our children feel everything intensely for the first time
and we marvel at the miracle of life.

Let us teach them to be warriors of compassion
with themselvesas well as the world around them.
Let us teach them to be guardians of the earth,
as well as one another.

I wish to lift their spirit and confidence,
with supportive, empowering words, actions and songs of praise.

I pray to encourage my child to explore what feels right to them,
and discover their authentic truths in this world for themselves.
To remind my child of their brilliance
and power to manifest dreams every new day,
especially in moments where they most need reminding that
- even if there are things that upset me sometimes -
I love them always, and they are still pure and shan't be shamed.

In this way, may my child never be afraid
to be open about the truth of their feelings and experience.
May they trust that I will be wise enough to respond with an open heart
and with the unconditional love they deserve and need,
even if they tell me something that initially feels difficult or painful.
I pray to never judge or scorn my child
for the challenging aspects of their experience,
but instead to guide them through their challenges.
I pray that I will be a shining example of what it means to do ones best
and even in the harder times,
to speak with honesty, integrity, and love with open arms.

Panacea Poetry by Bethany

Reuben
age 3
♡

In Dark Times We Can Be The Light

And where I fail, or make mistakes, or am not perfect
- because none of us can or will be -
I will also teach my child that its okay not to be perfect.
It is about the efforts we apply, a perspective of forgiveness,
learning from mistake
and loving ourselves not only when we shine,
but in our darker times.

Angels, teach me and guide me to be the mother my heart so yearns to be.
Allow me to nurture this beautiful, unique star-child
the universe gifted to me,
and teach me new levels of love.

May these lessons be passed to my child in time too
- forever encoded in their biofield, heart, mind, soul and Akashic records,
as well as the memories which forge a sacred bond between us,
a bond forged before I even birthed you, beautiful, perfect star-child
who has blessed this earth in human-form for a powerful, divine purpose.

Panacea Poetry by Bethany

Truest Love

Looking into a mirror,

do not seek imperfection.

Let your vision delight in beautiful details:

The soft pink of your lips, the contour of your jaw,

The sparkle in your eyes.

Sometimes others' untruthful cruelty

makes us feel inadequate,

But you are enough now and eternally.

You deserve appreciation.

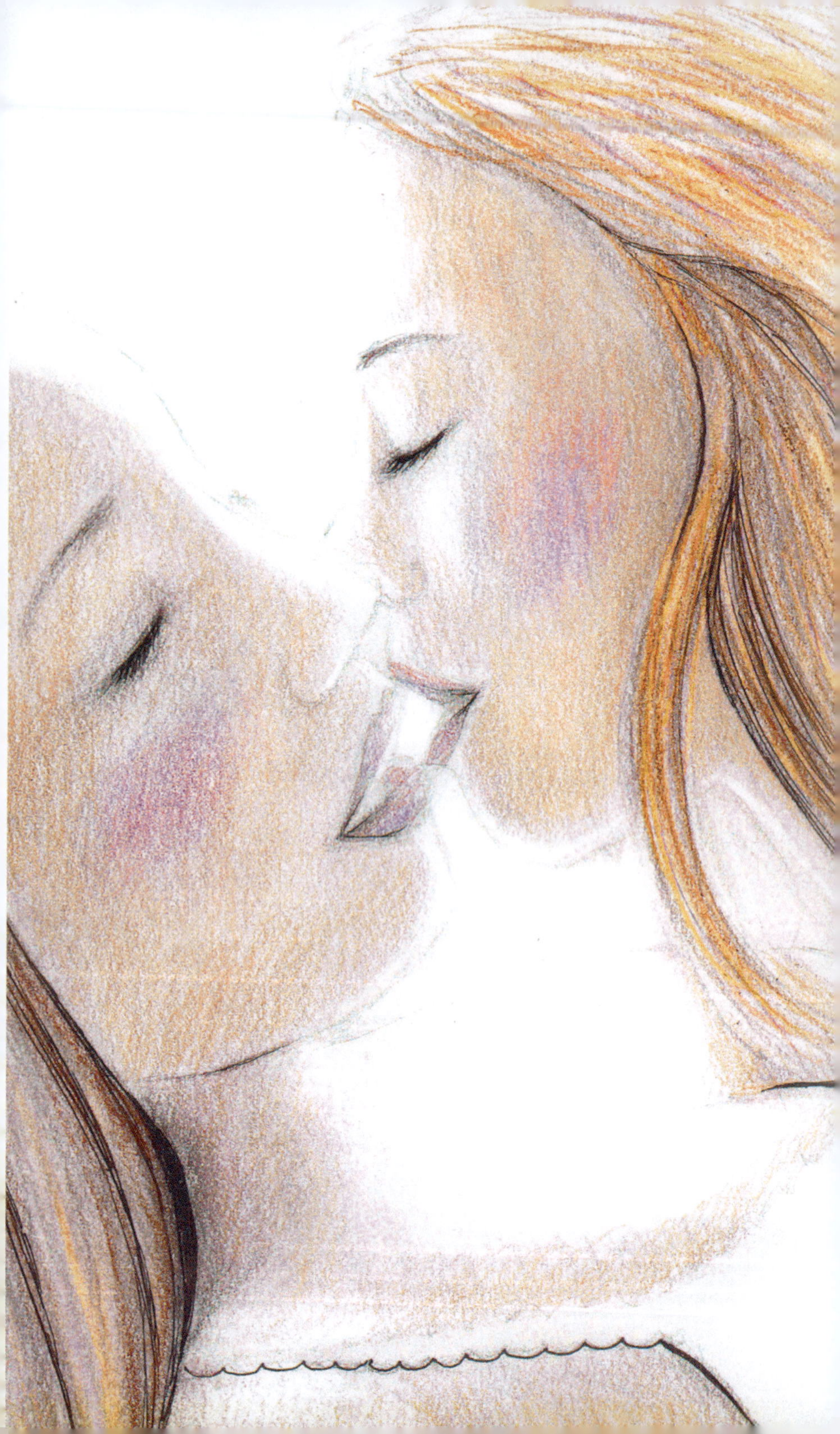

In Dark Times We Can Be The Light

You have always been lovable,

You must take distance from any

who make you feel inadequate,

for your own health and happiness.

You do not need to do anything,

be anything or change in any way

To be entirely lovable

and deserving of gentle nurturing.

The most powerful revolution

is not begun with fire, anger, or war,

but with a peaceful decision

to love in a kind, unconditional way.

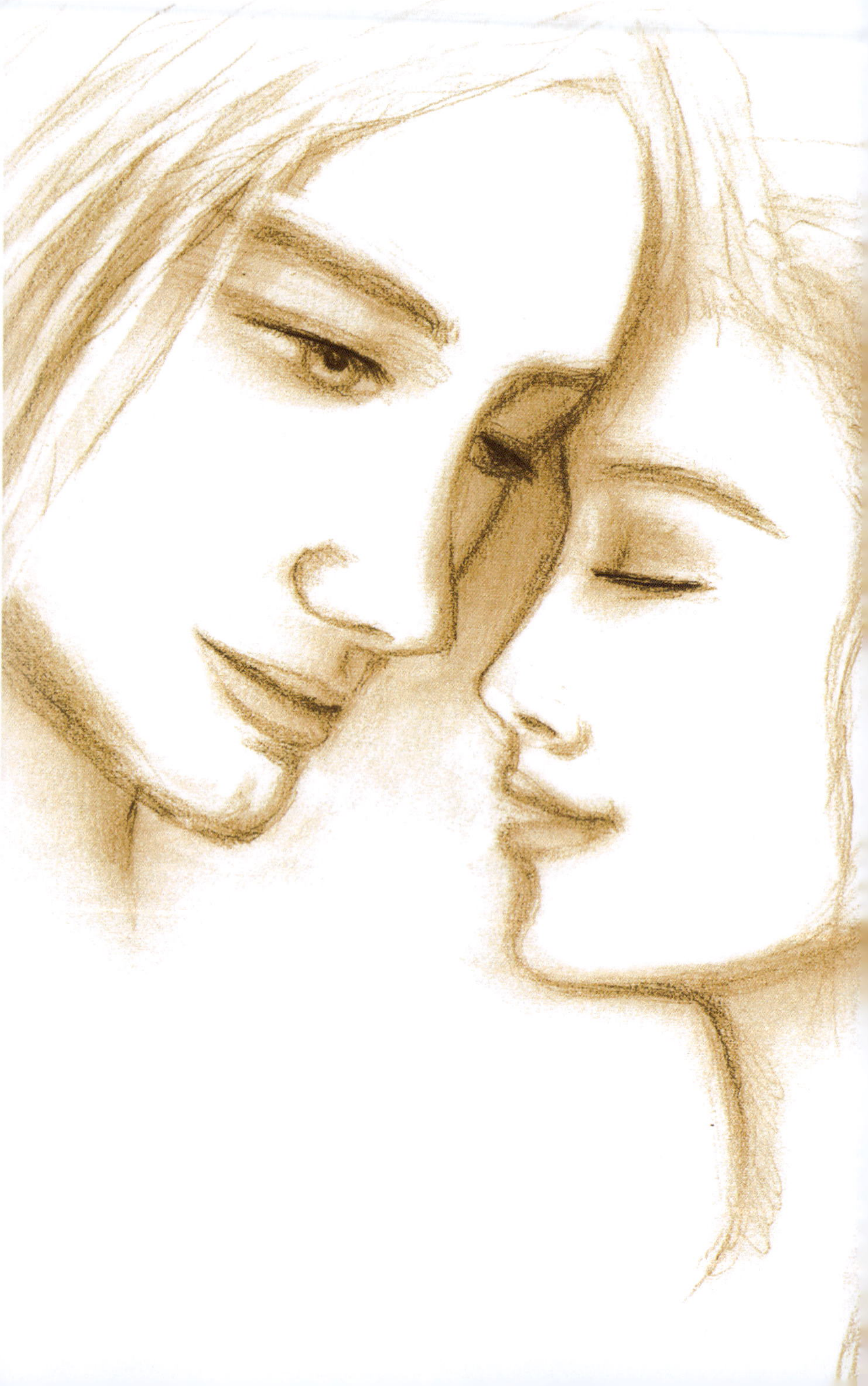

Truly Golden

In a world where so much costs money,

Where a payment seems necessary for so much,

There are some things that can always be free

Love, unconditional love

Empathy, kindness, gentleness, thoughtfulness,

The power of our own thoughts,

faith, choices moment to moment.

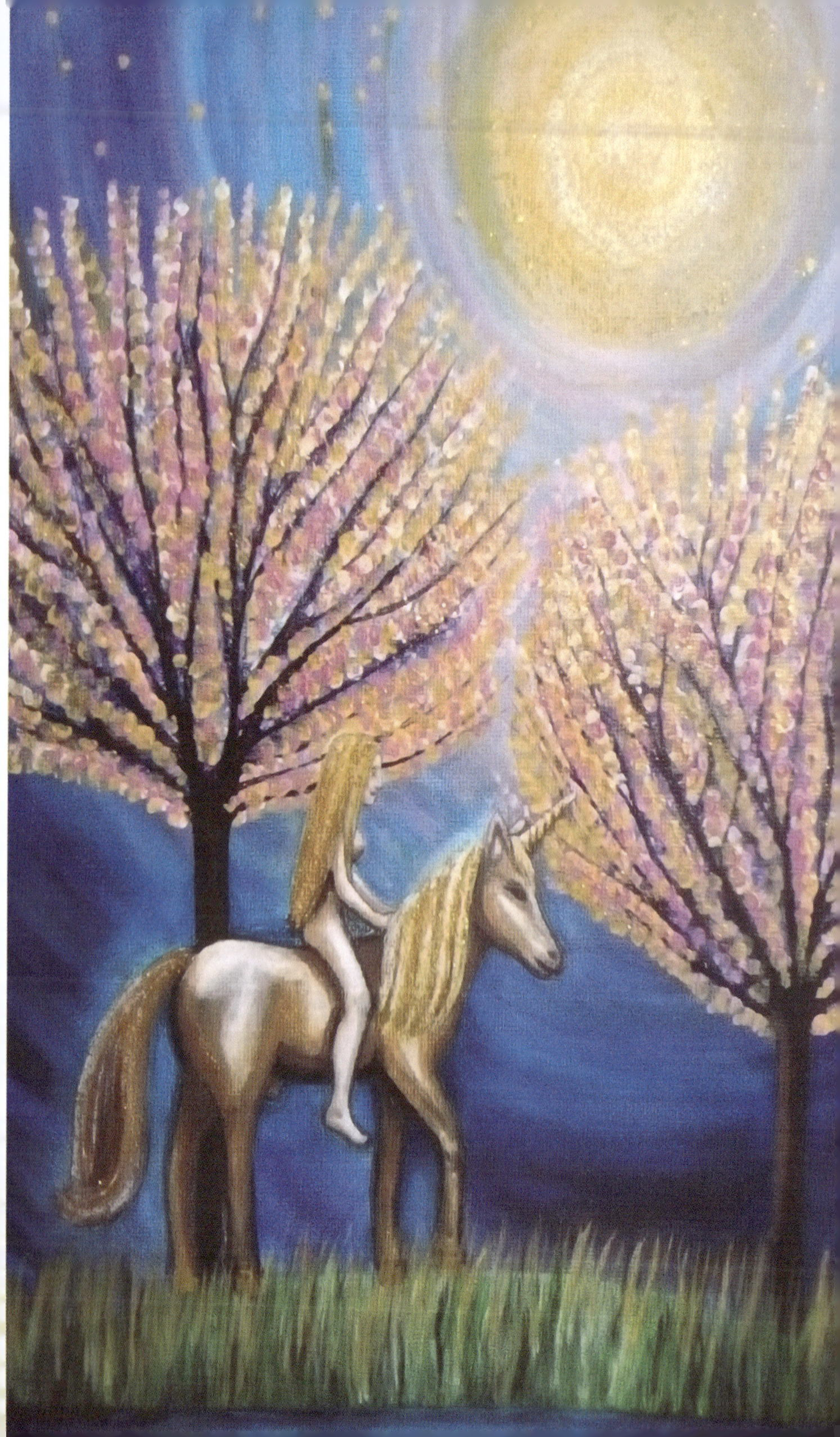

Part 2: Growing Up

Pestilence 67

Discordant 69

God Bless my Happy Nightmare 71

Mother 75

Mother & Daughter 77

Mum 79

Mother & Baby 81

2 Hearts 83

For My Brother: In Iambic Pentameter 85

Index of Paintings & Illustrations 87

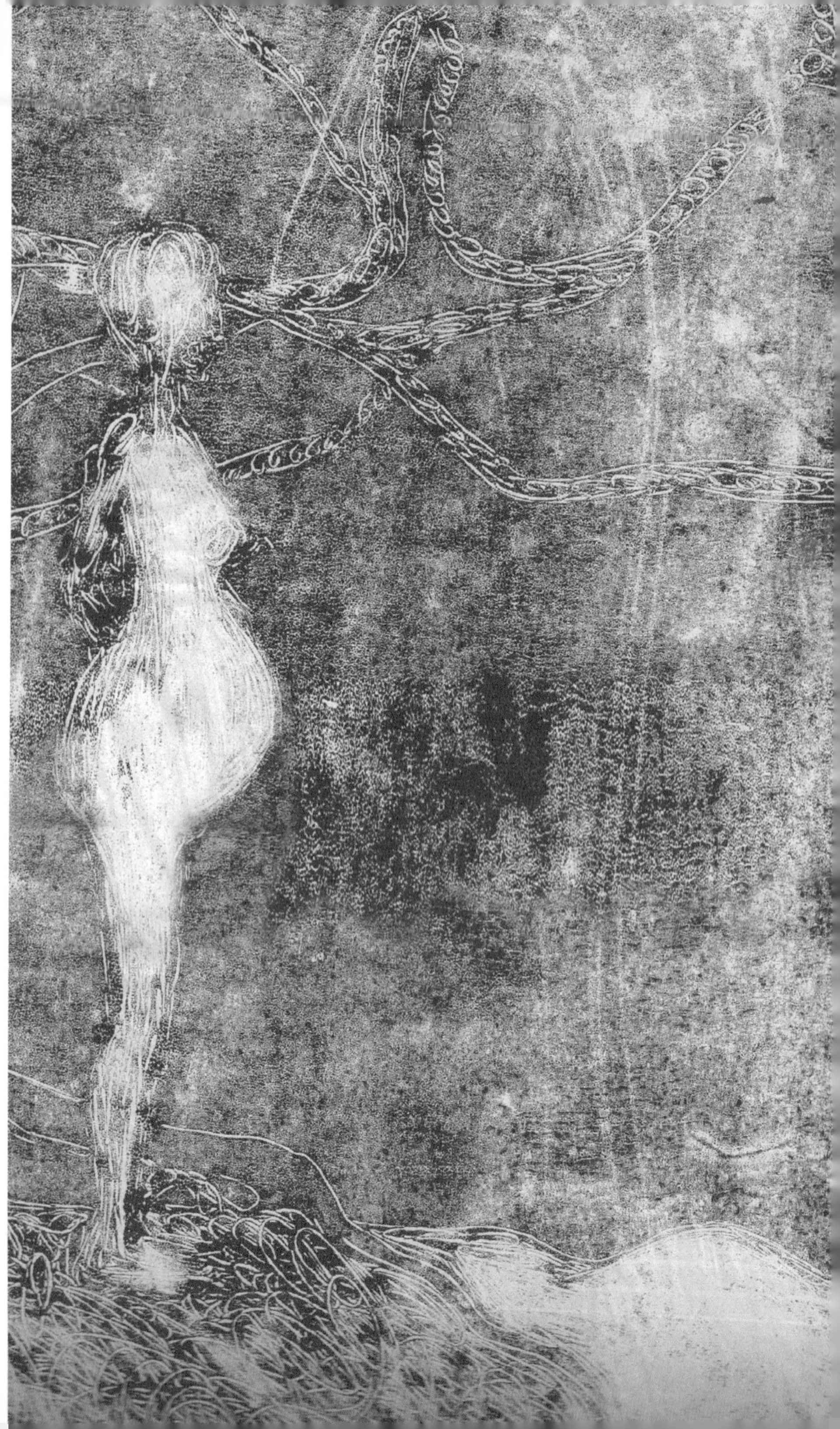

Pestilence

Children bawling, Mothers sprawling, Beggars calling,
No sense of who or whereabouts,
Face distorted, pale, livid...rigid -
Stares through eyes with no soul - gaping.

Gnawing pains on stomach, legs limp...I, not a part
Hoards stare through me, but a ghost,
As deadly murmurs fixate my ears,
Only one thought clear.

A whisper in mind churns through night,
For letter nought I write,
but tortured poetry as I take flight,
For my baby died this night,
The lost love in my life.

No strife did there used to be,
Just You, My Love, and me,
Then another entered, our child, my all,
Now my heart is crushed as she lies in dust.

But another I do carry,
One I cannot lose to famine,
Choosing to stay with You,
Would only be my future's downfall.

My lost all.

Panacea Poetry by Bethany

Discordant

I am ivory major, ebony minor,
Dissonance makes me yearn for finer,
Breaks in harmony, cracks in china.

I am sharp and always to scale,
I sing with high and quavered tail.
My tuned resound can never fail.

I don't play solos, only duets,
When I stand alone, silence begets,
I can't be wound, and I can't be set.

I lie ever silent in the dark,
Waiting for 'Maestro' to light a spark,
Yearning for my voice to fly like the lark.

My tonic was my heart song mate,
The music was passionate - yet he hurt me of late.
The conductor replaced me - at allegro rate.

Now my tone is no longer whole,
Without my consort, I have no goal.
I miss the tune within my soul.

Is this my finale?
My ending musicale?
My deceptive candencale?

I hear footsteps - ostinato score,
A door creaks - feet upon the floor,
A soft touch on my keys - Encore...

At last, Once More.

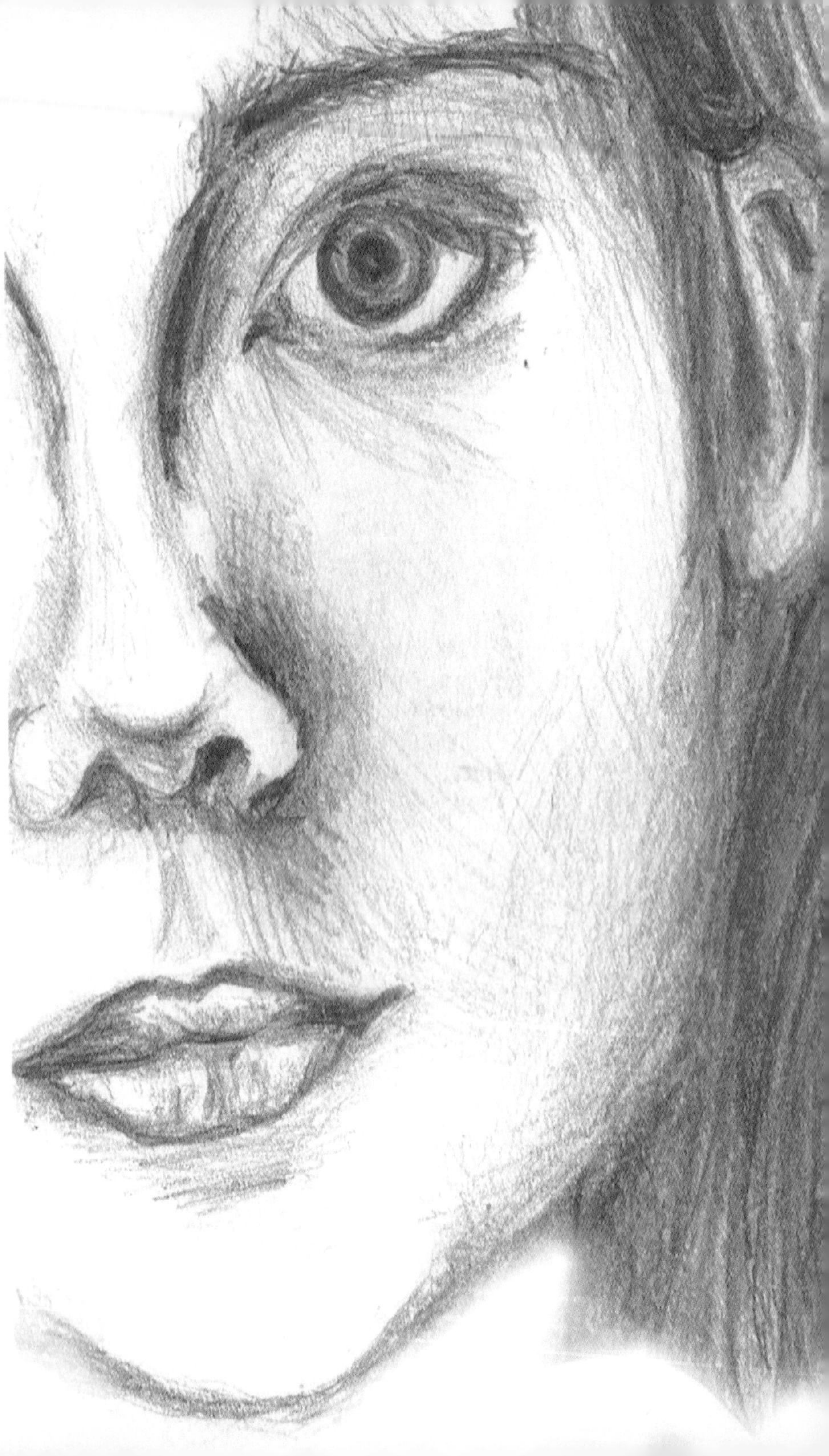

God Bless my *Happy* Nightmare

I'm running away to Land Freedom,

    where I feel safe- that's it.

I mean it, far away.

They say this *is* my home -

    but not with all the screams;

        breath, breathe: **the constant drumming.**

Not when the bottle cracks;

    -split sticky red over the table edge-

it's not a home when *I'm afraid.*

See me fall howling on my bed.

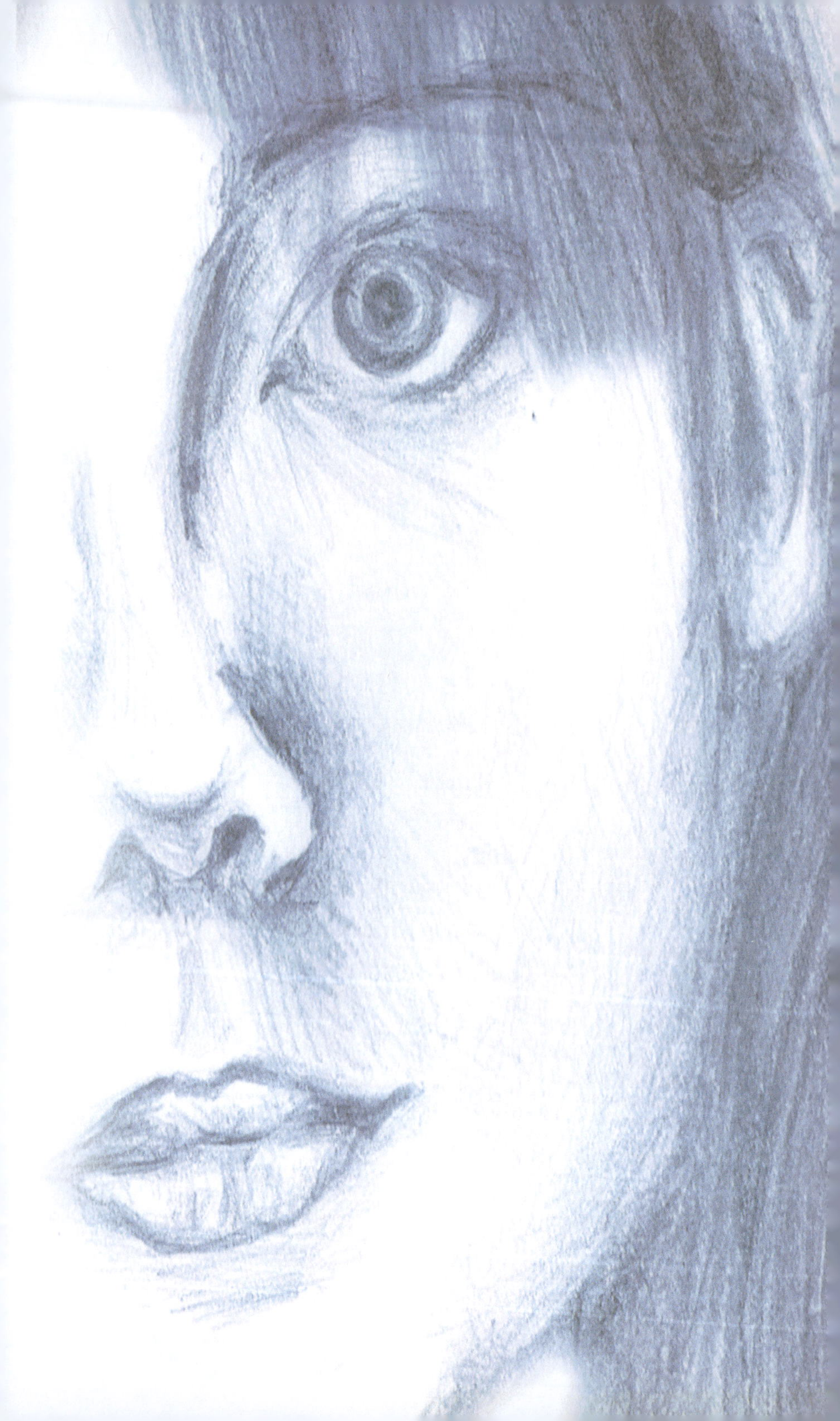

Tell me it's home when you're dreaming

of a life past it's boundaries:

where you'd be a legend. The free child.

'*So run,*' my mind whispers,

'*I dare you, I dare you.*'

Well I'm not a coward Papa: I **always** dared.

Goodbye my happy house on the hill,

I'm leaving behind your horrors,

look for me where your heart leads you Muma.

Call me. I'll always be home.

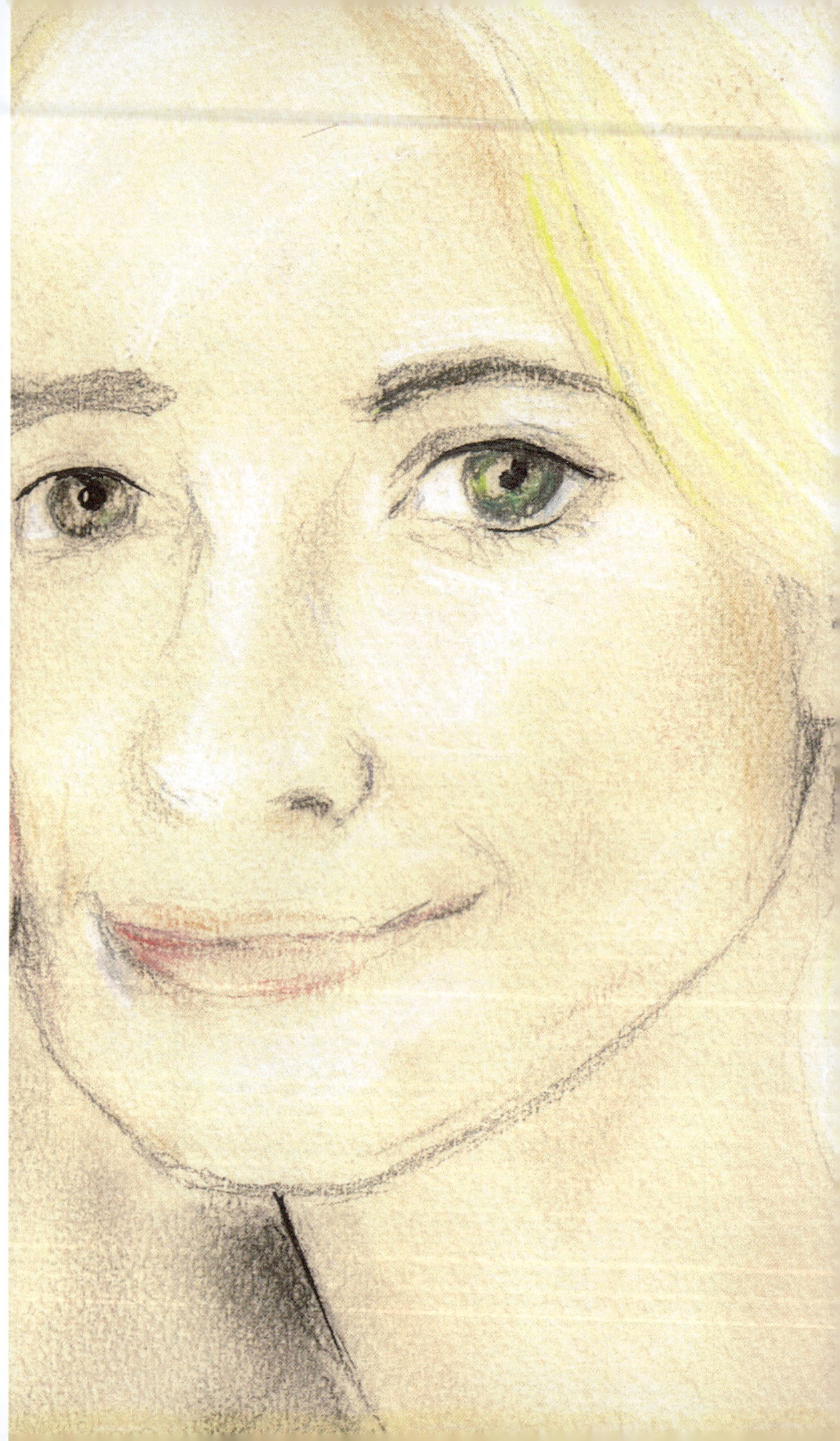

Mother

It makes my heart so sad to see

my mother thinks I am beauty

yet chooses always to ignore

the light which shines through her to us

is full of beauty & such strength

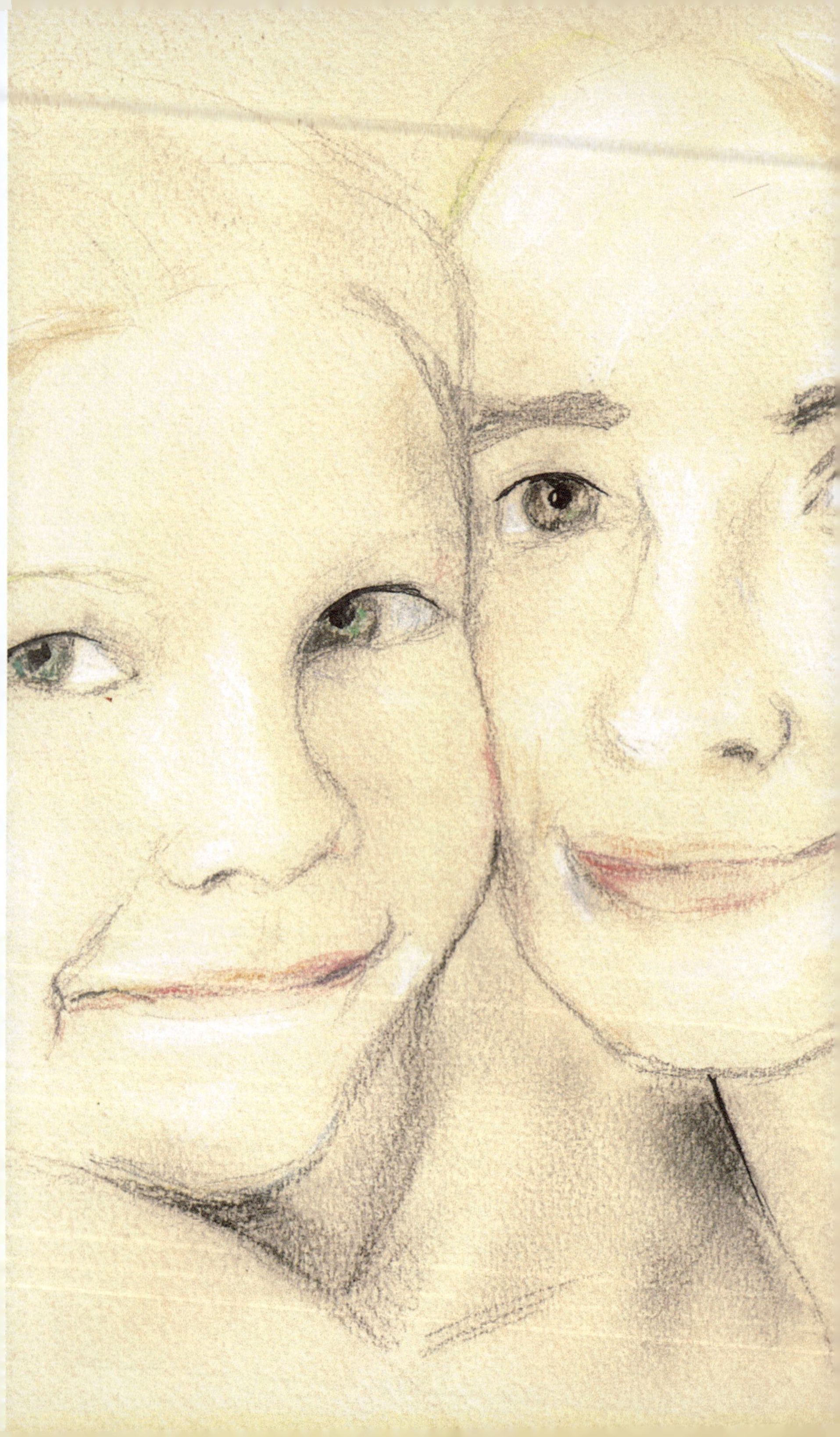

Mother & Daughter

My intuition tells me you are sad

As daughter I tell you do not lose hope.

Things are going to get better from now

And as long as we've got each other we'll cope

I promise always to be there for you;

May we both hold each other as we cry,

so when the new day dawns for both of us,

breathtaking smiles will light our faces again.

Panacea Poetry by Bethany

Mum

I caught sight of myself in the mirror,

& I thought I'd smile -

that was when I saw her,

the ghost of my mum in my features;

now I really smile <3

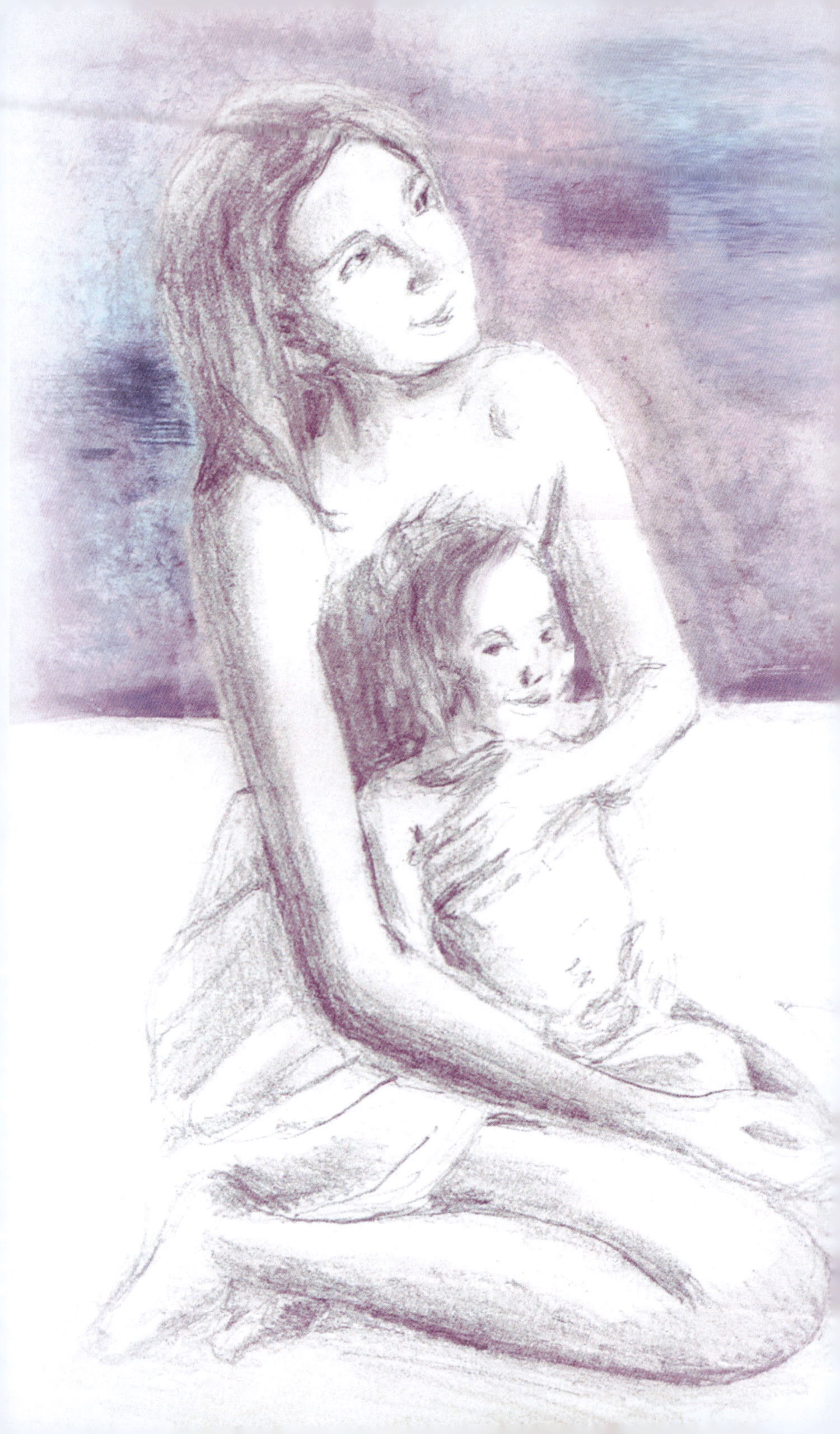

Mother & Baby

Don't take it on yourself
Please don't take offence
You know I think you're beautiful
And you always did your best

Please don't think I'm blaming you
No, I only meant to joke
You know you've been my lifesaver
And a ruby in the smoke.

You've held me up and held me cry
so please remember that.
I'll love you always
And anything that says otherwise

Is a lie

Is false

From this day forward
all my life
what we share
Still mother &baby
is too pure to be tarnished
by any foolish word
Now neither of us should feel guilt or sorrow
our bond too strong
to be hurt by a foolish word.

Panacea Poetry by Bethany

2 Hearts

Our hands - they are the same.

2 hearts in good places

a similar hue to our skin

the paths we walk are different

- confusion -

each one of us is lost.

But we have our loaf of bread.

We'll scatter crumbs as we walk

so neither of us is without the other.

And in the middle of the dark woods

with the bears, the gremlins and the wiches

we'll find a gingerbread house

and defeat the witch.

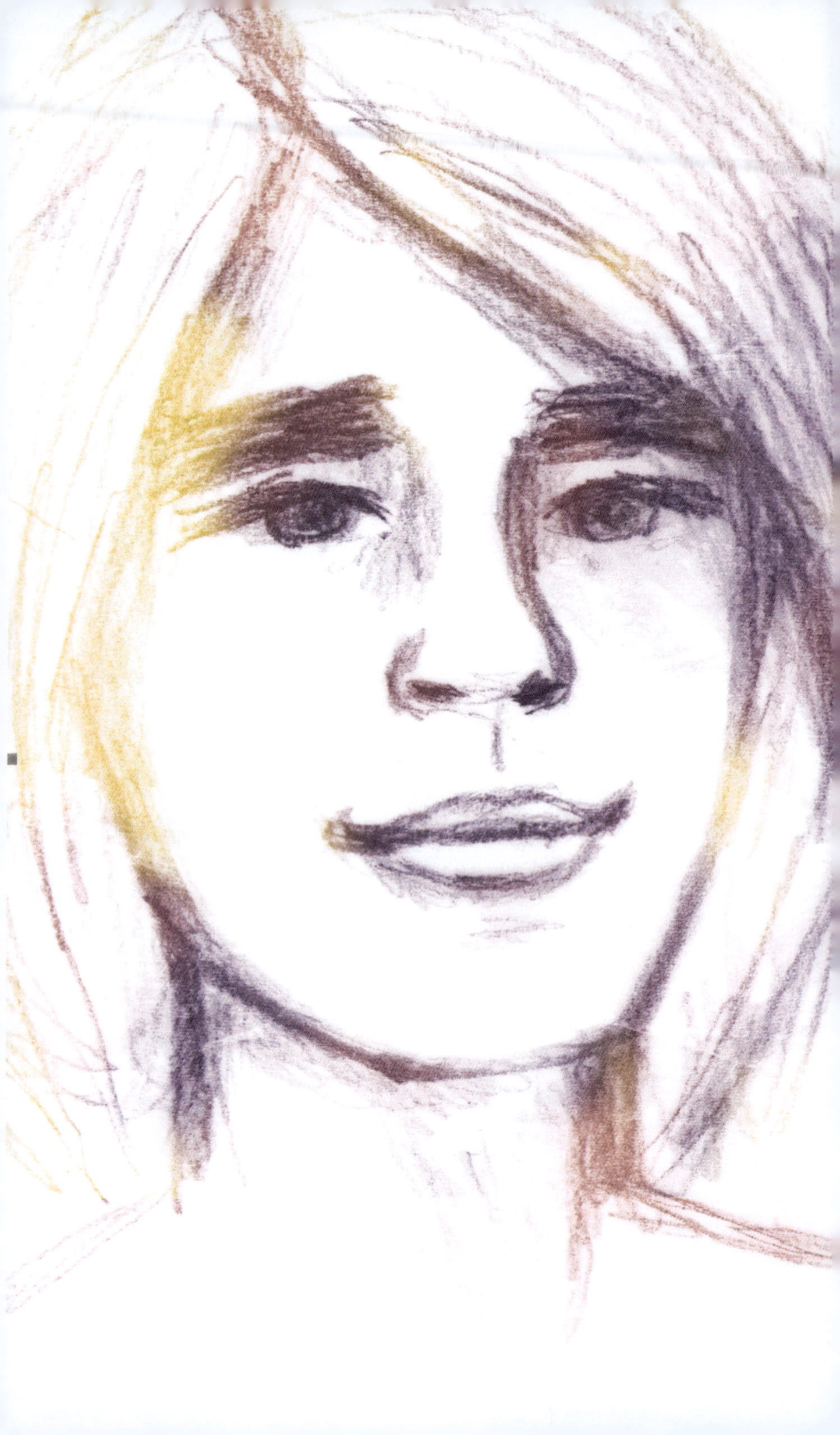

For My Brother:
In Iambic Pentameter

Shall I compare thee to a Summer's day?

When ambiance is more than one of four.

His youth and prospects bring the hope of May,

Then sharp wit leaves Spring's gentile most sore

And blunt manner doth echo Winter's way.

But clear to me he's most which I adore

An Autumn wind whose beauty life won't sway.

What brother more of God could I ask for.

Brings me joy to know I'll love him always.

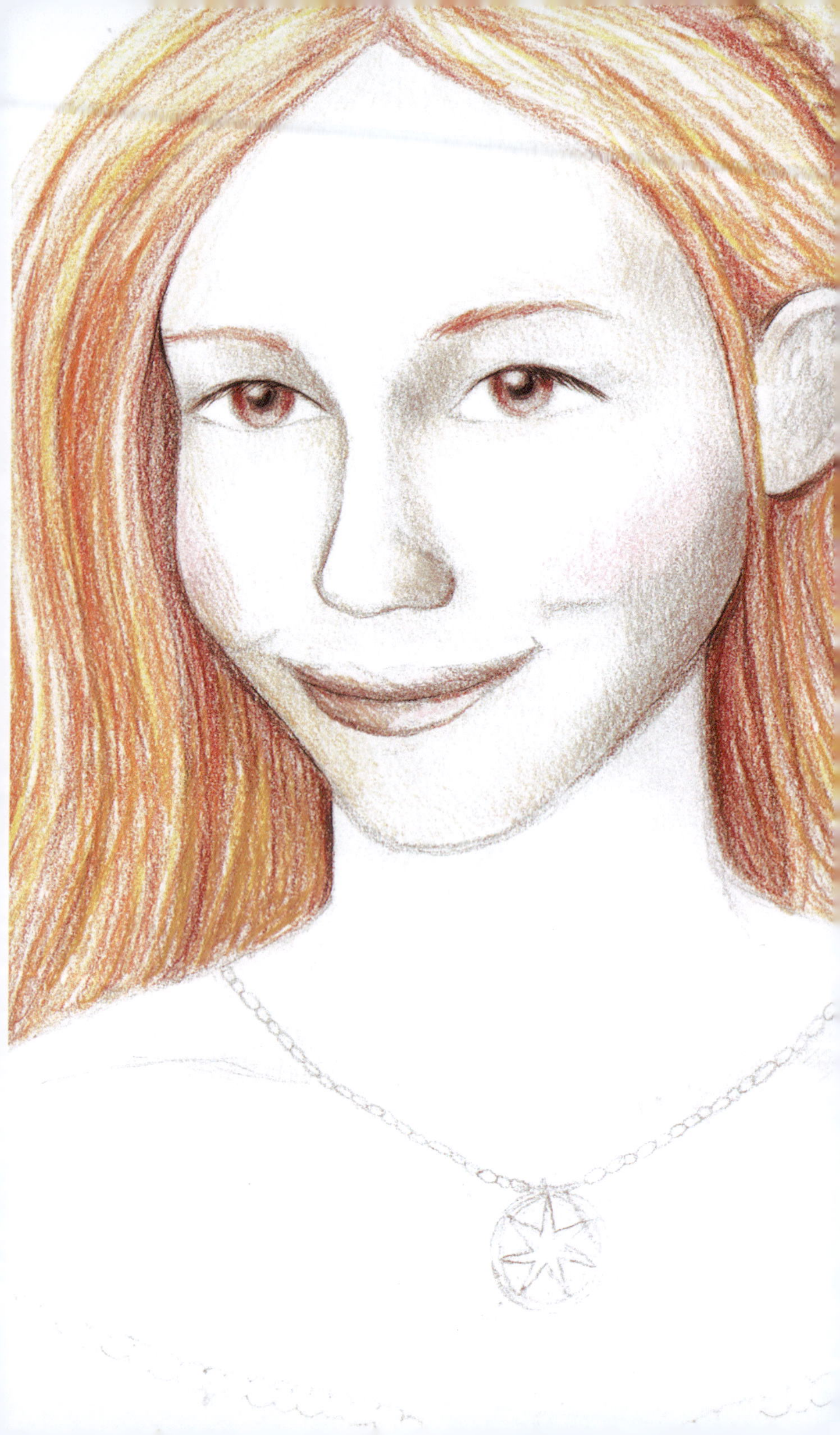

In Dark Times We Can Be The Light

Illustrations

Cover: 'Self-portrait age 17', oil - 2012
Title page: 'When Our Minds Meet, That Is When We Find Peace', graphite -2019
Dedication: 'Untitled', coloured pencil - 2016
Foreword: 'Beth' (by her mother), coloured pencil - 2019
Contents (1): From 'Tree Of Life' series, acrylic - 2018
Introduction: 'Expressions Of Love', coloured pencil - 2018
Art: 'Study of Adam and Eve by Raphael', graphite and watercolour - 2012
The Beauty of Human Form: 'Exploring Contrast, Light & Dark, Male & Female', graphite -2018
Lucidity: 'Self-portrait age 14', pen and ink with gouache - 2008
Pandemic of Spiritual Amnesia: From 'Tree Of Life' series, acrylic - 2018
Oasis: 'Untitled', gouache - date unknown
Oasis: 'Double Portrait Of Two Girls', graphite - 2011
Birth: Divine Origins: 'Untitled', gouache - 2011
Birth: Divine Origins: 'Divine Origins', gouache - 2012
Soul: 'Naked Couple', graphite - 2018
Shattered Illusions: 'Drowning In Internal Screams', pen and ink - 2010
The Reality of Perfection: 'I'm Home When I'm With You', graphite - 2018
Karmic Knot: 'Exploring Light & Shade, Shape & Curve', graphite - 2018
Lies: 'Exploring Different Colour Tones', soft pastel - 2012
Lies: 'Samson & The Lion', coloured pencil - 2017
Lies: 'Untitled', graphite, coloured pencil & watercolour - date unknown
Lies: 'Not All Beauty Is Society's Convention' (1), coloured pencil - 2017
Lovable: 'Not All Beauty Is Society's Convention' (2), coloured pencil - 2017
Lovable: 'Fae Is Your World', graphite - 2018
The Lamb Transformed To Wolf: 'The Lamb Transformed To Wolf', graphite - 2018
The Lamb Transformed To Wolf: 'Ecstasy Within One Another', graphite - 2018
Awareness: 'Madonna', graphite and bodycolour -2018
The Riddle of Multiple Truths: 'Untitled', coloured pencil - 2016
Mother's Prayer: 'Reuben Age 3' -2017
Truest Love: 'Gentle Romance', coloured pencil - 2018
Truly Golden: 'Kiss Me Like You Want Me Forever', graphite - 2019
Contents (2): From 'Tree Of Life' series, acrylic - 2018
Pestilence: 'Untitled', lino print - 2012
Discordant: 'Beth Playing Piano', (by her mother) graphite - 2011
God Bless My Happy Nightmare: 'Self-portrait age 14', graphite - 2008
Mother: 'Mother And Daughter', pastel - date unknown
Mother & Daughter: 'Mother And Daughter', pastel - date unknown
Mum: 'Mother And Daughter', pastel - date unknown
Mother & Baby: 'Mother and Child', graphite and watercolour - 2012
2 Hearts: 'Mother and Child', graphite and watercolour - 2012
For My Brother: In Iambic Pentameter: 'Untitled', graphite, 2018
This page (verso): 'Lyra', coloured pencil, 2018
This page (recto): 'Deer Spirit', graphite and coloured pencil, 2018
Final page: 'I'm Home When I'm With You', graphite - 2018

'I'm home when I'm with you'

Printed in Great Britain
by Amazon